The Little Self-Esteem Workbook

The Little Workbooks Series

The Little ACT Workbook

The Little Anxiety Workbook

The Little CBT Workbook

The Little Depression Workbook

The Little Mindfulness Workbook

The Little Self-Esteem Workbook

The Little Stress-Relief Workbook

The Little
Self-Esteem
Workbook

Boost your confidence and get more out of life

Samantha Carbon

crimson

Important note
The information in this book is not intended as a substitute for medical advice.
Neither the author nor Hachette UK can accept any responsibility for any injuries,
damages or losses suffered as a result of following the information herein.

First published in Great Britain in 2021 by Crimson
An imprint of Hodder & Stoughton
An Hachette UK company

1

A CIP catalogue record for this title is available from the British Library

Trade Paperback ISBN 978 1 78059282 4
eBook ISBN 978 1 78059283 1

Typeset in Whitney HTF by Hewer Text UK Ltd, Edinburgh
Printed and bound in Great Britain by Clays Ltd, Elcograf S.p.A.

Hodder & Stoughton policy is to use papers that are natural, renewable and recyclable
products and made from wood grown in sustainable forests. The logging and manufacturing
processes are expected to conform to the environmental regulations of the country of origin.

Hodder & Stoughton Ltd
Carmelite House
50 Victoria Embankment
London EC4Y 0DZ

www.hodder.co.uk

Contents

About the author

Samantha Carbon is a London-based psychotherapist, clinical supervisor and coach. She is the founder of Samantha Carbon Therapy and Baker Street Therapy. With over a decade's involvement in the psychotherapy field, she has made tremendous contributions to this industry. Samantha holds a Master's degree in Psychotherapy from the renowned Metanoia Institute in London. She is a relational therapist supporting individuals in reducing their stress, anxieties, addictions and other presentations. As a compassionate professional, she supports individuals from diverse backgrounds to embrace their sense of difference. Samantha has written for numerous publications including the *Huffington Post*, *Psychologies*, the *Daily Telegraph* and *Stylist*, among others. She has authored and published two other books: *All That Glitters* (2010) and *Sons and Daughters: A View to Understanding Transgender Issues* (2017).

Introduction

Welcome to *The Little Self-Esteem Workbook,* in which I hope to help you through the periods of unhappiness that come when we suffer from low self-esteem. If you have picked up this book, you might relate to some of the following:

- You often have a negative opinion of yourself

- You judge or evaluate yourself harshly

- You struggle to acknowledge your positive qualities and characteristics

- You are, at times, dissatisfied with the way you are and where you are in life

- You may be inclined to feel like a failure

- Perhaps you feel emotionally drained from addressing these issues

You are not alone – these are common issues for many people. Life is constantly changing and it's a challenge to stay on an even keel. Your self-esteem comes from many different areas of life, from how you think you look, to how your clothes feel, to whether you think you are a 'success' and how you imagine the world views you. And just as it comes from all these different areas, so it affects them in return. So, what if I was to tell you that maintaining or improving your self-esteem is vital for your own health and wellbeing?

I imagine you'd wonder how and why.

Working on your self-esteem can support you to have a positive opinion of yourself. It can:

- ease the internal dialogue that lives within you

- encourage you to see your qualities

- help you embrace who and where you are in life

This book is going to support you to understand your self-esteem and the ways in which how you feel about yourself ties in with living a fuller and happier life. The strategies and exercises in this book will support you to shed some light on your level of self-esteem and they will give you some insight into the kind of personal struggles you may be facing.

Many people feel bad about themselves from time to time. For some, it may be very difficult to feel upbeat when they're under pressure or when they're experiencing emotions that are challenging to manage. There are times when people might feel drawn into a downward spiral of negative thoughts and feelings.

There are many reasons for a person to have low self-esteem, and some of those reasons can be extremely complex. A person may have gone through a very traumatic event and, as a result, they've lost all sense of who they are. Someone may have a low body image, where it affects their self-esteem to the point where they don't want to leave the house. Furthermore, another person might have been bullied in school and the ramifications of this may mean they feel terrified attending social events in their adult years. Does any of the above sound familiar?

Low self-esteem can be a constant companion, especially for those who experience depression, anxiety, stress or phobias. When you feel down, when you feel like your self-worth is almost at sub-zero levels, nothing feels right. People with optimum levels of self-esteem are aware of the inner realities that support them to be more self-compassionate and more available to others. By contrast, people with low self-esteem can be lost in life, lacking in energy and weakened by their existence.

It can be hard to fully identify your level of self-esteem because your feelings fluctuate from day to day. One day you may be feeling great about yourself and then on the next feelings of self-doubt flood in. Events can affect the way you feel, as well as your confidence levels and the way you view the world, but all of this can be changed if you choose to see things differently.

When your self-esteem increases, everything in life appears to feel better. New possibilities, experiences and opportunities can be achieved and you generally lean towards the positive. You feel healthier, happier, and your relationships and friendships flourish. When you may have stayed home before, you now feel inclined to go out. When you might have failed to take a work opportunity in the past, you're now ready and raring to go. Is this something you want for yourself?

How to Use this Book

This book can help you understand more about self-esteem and identify what your level of self-esteem is in the here and now. From there, I'll help you to improve it in a slow and steady manner. Of course, self-esteem sways throughout a lifetime, even over a year or a month. When you are not doing so well, it will register low and when you're feeling better, it will likely register higher. So, it's important to understand that a certain amount of fluctuation is normal.

I encourage you to use the blank spaces within the exercise boxes to write down whatever comes to mind. Having a greater sense of self-esteem arms you against the storms of anxiety and worry, and the easy exercises and opportunities to write will help you. Recording your journey through this book will show you your progress and reflections.

As you work through some of the exercises, many changes will be set in motion, so please be kind to yourself in this process. If some of the questions are triggering, all I ask of you is to observe and note the process as it unfolds.

I like to work directly on problem-solving behaviours and supporting clients to develop day-to-day tools for finding constructive,
creative solutions when they are experiencing challenges with
self-esteem. So, look out for the exercises in which I encourage
you to **Stop**, **Reflect** and **Feel** where you are in that moment.
What do I mean by **Stop**, **Reflect** and **Feel**? I want you to pause,
think about what's going on in your mind and pay attention to how
you are feeling *in that moment*.

Now you may not have capacity to **Reflect** and **Feel**, however, this
is about hitting the pause button for these moments so you can
take in where you are and how you are feeling. This awareness of
the present will act as a foundation, which is why we cover it in
Chapter 1 on **Mindfulness**.

The strategies in this book will support you to shed some light on
your level of self-esteem and they will give you insights into the
kind of personal struggles you may be facing. It will be helpful to
understand where your low self-esteem may stem from. This, in
itself, will allow you to move forward and develop your self-esteem
levels further. To help you understand, I will use fictional examples
throughout, illustrating how low self-esteem shows up. The exercises will support you to connect the dots, which we seldom do,

even though many of our present-day challenges with self-esteem are connected to our earlier conditioning. The commitment to doing the exercises can yield tremendous results.

As with any self-development journey, the results are cumulative. That means they're going to build up slowly and then one day you'll look back and realise that all that work was worth it because you suddenly feel a lot stronger. We cover this in Chapter 2 on **Comfort, Stretch, Panic**. This is so that you may recognise how your self-esteem has moved along the scale, but it won't happen straight away.

The theme of compassion flows throughout this book. It will give you greater clarity because personal failings can be acknowledged with kindness. Many early relationships and experiences will form the basis of your self-esteem, so we will reflect on what your childhood was like, along with the early messages you received. This isn't intended to unearth anything difficult, but to simply allow you to understand why your self-esteem may be a little on the low side. Many children are told they can't do anything or, equally damaging, are told they 'should' be able to do absolutely anything with ease. This notion can place a lot of pressure on many people. We will explore childhood in detail in Chapter 3.

So, are you ready to give yourself permission to consider new thoughts, feelings and behaviours? There will be many of these as you progress through the book, so please encourage yourself to **Stop**, **Reflect** and **Feel** where you are when you are doing the exercises and writing in your journal. You will learn a variety of self-esteem enhancing skills that you can call upon whenever you feel like your self-esteem could do with a boost. Some exercises you may feel you only need to do once, others may be worth revisiting time and again.

Before we get into the book, I need to point out one very important thing: you will not notice results overnight, so let's tame the inner critic that lives in your head which we will get to know in Chapter 4. Please do not become disheartened if after day one of your new mission you don't feel different. This is not a race, it is something you need to commit to and wait for the results to snowball into something notable.

In knowing your capabilities and your weaknesses, you can learn that setbacks and disappointments are neither permanently damaging nor diminishing. They are part of personal growth experiences and that in itself is empowering. You will get to know your true self in Chapter 5, and to recognise you are powerful and wonderful in your own way – you are unique.

These practices are about building up your self-esteem to become emotionally strong, empowered and understanding of your limitations, which we cover in **Boundaries** in Chapter 6. It's about your getting to know yourself and developing the kind of character that makes you clear and honest about who you are along with what you want for you. We explore in Chapter 7 the **Powerful Messages** we have grown up with. By going through these exercises, you will become your own best friend and perhaps the only person who understands your own true complexities.

Reading this book may well prompt you to work on all of these strategies, or you may choose a few which call out to you. It's a good idea to examine them all, however, as you might not know at this point what is going to work and what might be less successful. A mixture of a few could be a good starting point, or if it suits you to concentrate on them one at a time instead, that's perfectly fine too. Chapter 8 on **Building Healthy Self-Esteem** will be a gentle reminder on the importance of self-esteem and the hope is that you don't abandon the process and return to life as you know it. Remember, there is no one-size-fits-all answer here, it's really what connects with you personally. Working with this book you will experience an intensive guided encounter with yourself especially when we explore **Social Media and Anxiety** in Chapter 9.

Remember – a steady approach is a successful approach, so take your time. Understand each point before you move on, and commit your time and effort to making a real difference in your life. Once self-esteem starts to rise, it's an unstoppable force and a very powerful one.

My Approach

In my private practice, I use an integrative approach which brings together different theories and models from a variety of humanistic, psychoanalytic and cognitive concepts. I lean more towards the Transactional Analysis model, which has been designed to promote personal growth and change.

Let me explain that a little more deeply. The Transactional Analysis modality was developed by Eric Berne, a psychiatrist in the 1950s. A key principle within this modality is that we are all born 'OK' and that we can change. At any time we may adopt one of four 'life positions', which are how we see, feel or think in relation to ourselves and others:

1. I'm Okay, You're Okay – People in this position have positive experiences with others. They can solve

problems and they realise the significance of others being in their life.

2. I'm Not Okay, You're Okay – People in this position believe and feel that others are doing things better; they may feel inferior and have the belief others can do more; they lean towards being dissatisfied with themselves.

3. I'm Okay, You're Not Okay – People in this position are of the belief that they are right and others around them are wrong. They are likely to put blame on others.

4. I'm Not Okay, You're Not Okay – People in this position often lack interest in their environment or surroundings whether it is their family, work or social group and they generally don't want to take part in making changes for themselves.

They may sound simple but they're a great starting point when I am working with my clients. Many will come into therapy in the position of 'I'm Not Okay' and part of the work is getting them to the position of 'I'm Okay'.

As humans we don't stay in one position all the time, and if our self-esteem is being challenged we may shift between positions minute by minute. Throughout the book, I will refer to these 'life positions' to demonstrate how individuals see themselves and how they exist in the rest of the world.

I believe that past life events can hold the key to understanding what present difficulties you may be experiencing and I encourage you to consider which 'life position' relates to you at different times in your story. Throughout the book you will come across a range of different strategies that aim to support more rational thinking and challenging of those pesky limiting beliefs. We all have them, but they *can* be changed!

Before we begin with our first chapter, let me just say that I am so pleased you have reached out and you're starting to consider your own needs. Focusing on your self-esteem is never a waste of time, it's a lifelong necessity. By doing so, you're investing in your wellbeing and happiness.

My hope is your awareness will be a source of support throughout this book. My invitation to you is to use this book as a license to change how you experience yourself.

Let's begin!

Part 1

What is Self-Esteem?

1 Self-Esteem

Self-esteem is a term that is used to describe what you consider to be your value or your self-worth. If you don't believe that you're valuable, e.g. you feel worthless, your self-esteem is very low. However, if you have a high level of self-worth, chances are you have a high level of self-esteem. If you are reading this book on self-esteem, it's probably safe to say that your self-esteem is not in an okay place.

The American Psychological Association defines self-esteem as:

'The degree to which the qualities and characteristics contained in one's self-concept are perceived to be positive. It reflects a person's physical self-image, view of his or her accomplishments and capabilities, and values and perceived success in living up to them, as well as how others view and respond to that person.'

Putting yourself at the top of your own priority list can be extremely difficult at first. This is because we're told from a very young age that we need to be considerate of others and put their needs before our own. But that's not necessarily the case all the time. If you don't look after yourself, how can you be the best version of yourself?

When you start putting your own needs first, it will probably feel alien, simply because it's something you may have been avoiding for many years.

Of course, when it comes to focusing on number one, there is a certain amount of moderation we need to exercise. You can't go around focusing on yourself and not thinking about anyone else all the time; in that case, yes you may be viewed as a tad selfish. However, when you apply these rules in moderation you will realise that it's entirely possible to put yourself first and not feel guilty about it, while also being able to help others around you, simply because you're a stronger, happier and healthier version of you. How can there be anything negative in that?

One way to see self-esteem is on a continuum or meter, with low being at one end and high at the other.

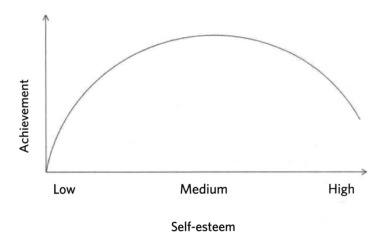

One point to consider: in different environments the meter will fluctuate just like your self-esteem. As you work through this book there will be opportunities to reflect on the continuum. It is important to note that both high and low levels can be emotionally and socially challenging for the individual if there is no awareness.

What do I mean by high? Many people adopt a 'mask' in order to survive their environments at any given time; perhaps they're going through a rough time at work or they're struggling in their relationship. They don't want to show it to the outside world. They may show up with what seems like oodles of self-esteem – however, when they run out of energy, the mask may slip and the truth may be exposed, which can be extremely challenging for that particular individual.

There is no doubt that low self-esteem can be problematic and often lead to depression and a lack of motivation. However, trying to always have a high level of self-esteem can also be exhausting and can lead to burn-out. It's about finding an even keel, a fair balance between the two states, which doesn't cause you to always be negative and down but which doesn't put you under undue pressure to be constantly happy and sunny.

So, you could say that an optimum level of self-esteem is located in the middle of the continuum. Can you **Stop**, **Reflect** and **Feel** where you are on the continuum? Place a dot where you would you like to be by the end of this book.

As you go through this book, I invite you to adopt a less black-and-white way of thinking and sit more in the grey area in the middle. That sounds easy, right? Well, it's not going to be at first. I invite you to change your default setting and see things in a slightly different way to what you've been used to. That in itself can be a challenge, but it's one which can be conquered. Ultimately by going through this book, you will understand your levels of self-esteem without looking to others, because only you can do you. Only you know how you feel. So, avoid comparing yourself with others because, as I shared before, many people wear masks to defend and disguise their moments of low self-esteem.

As we work through this book, I invite you to identify your emotions. I have provided a list to get started with. This exercise will be useful to recognise the emotions you are familiar with, as well as the ones you are not. Some of these emotions will show up when your self-esteem is not in a great place.

Exercise 1.1

Emotion valley

Circle the emotions that you relate to in this present moment:

Amazed Angry Annoyed Anxious Ashamed Bitter Bored Comfortable Confused Content Depressed Determined Disdainful Disgusted Eager Embarrassed Energetic Envious Excited Foolish Frustrated Furious Grieving Happy Hopeful Hurt Inadequate Insecure Inspired Irritated Jealous Joyful Lonely Lost Loving Miserable Motivated Nervous Overwhelmed Peaceful Proud Relieved Resentful Sad Satisfied Scared Self-conscious Shocked Silly Stupid Suspicious Tense Terrified Trapped Uncomfortable Worried Worthless

Exercise 1.2

Your motivations

Am I right that something has prompted you to invest your time in this book? Perhaps the subject of self-esteem has been on your mind for some time, in which case give yourself a round of applause for taking the first steps. What were the emotions you experienced when you purchased or picked up this book? And why? List as many as you can.

(Example: I felt sad and envious because my colleague was given a promotion which I wanted and deserved.)

_____

_____

_____

_____

_____

_____

Awareness

When you were writing about how you felt in that exercise, how did it feel? For some of you it probably felt odd at first, but the more you do this, the easier it will become to reflect openly and honestly. Many people find writing down their emotions difficult at first, but over time it becomes a cathartic process, something they rely upon as an outlet. So, even if it feels strange at first, please stick with it.

As we continue, hold all your feelings about your self-esteem with kindness, because the concept of self-esteem is not written in stone. I invite you to be in your 'conscious state' when you are looking at your self-esteem. What do I mean by being in your conscious state? I invite you to be aware of your sensations, your thoughts, your surroundings. Having this awareness requires living in the here and now, and not in the elsewhere, the past or the future. The awareness of your self-esteem is an important step towards achieving your goals. So, as you begin to gain awareness of the impact of your low self-esteem, please don't be discouraged. Getting to understand your levels of self-esteem is a process. It is not something that is just going to click into place simply because you've decided to address it. This book is designed for you to see yourself more clearly and accurately in the here and now and you are encouraged not to ignore, distort or hide your personal shortcomings as they arise. We all have shortcomings.

Eric Berne, author of *The Games People Play* said: 'Awareness means the capacity to see a coffee pot and hear the birds sing in one's way, and not the way one was taught'. So, what does he mean by this? Children see and hear things differently from their parents and caregivers; take the scenario below:

Young boy: Dad, can you hear the birds?
Dad: Yes son, there is a robin and a sparrow.
Young boy: Is there?

The moment that the little boy is concerned with which bird is a robin and which is a sparrow, he can no longer see the birds or hear them sing. Many people see and hear in the ways that have been taught to them versus what they have learnt for themselves.

Mindfulness

Are you familiar with mindfulness? Mindfulness is the art of living in the present and appreciating the small things. This practice can support your happiness, boost your self-esteem and allow you to live your life without missing it because you're thinking about a million other things. How many times have you been sat on the bus or in your car in a traffic jam and your mind wanders? You start thinking about your to-do list, or start mulling over something that happened last week that you wish you'd done differently. As a result, you often miss the rainbow that's formed in front of you, or you miss the really cute dog that just ran past your car. The small things in life are what make it all worthwhile and you're missing them and living in your head.

By having the awareness of your own experiences in the current moment, mindfulness represents the opposite of experiential avoidance, which many people do when their self-esteem is low. Experiential avoidance is your attempt or desire to suppress your unwanted internal experiences, such as your memories, your thoughts, your emotions and your bodily sensations. In short, mindfulness can encourage you to be a personally and socially aware person, and a happier one, too.

Be honest, do you live in the past? Are you always lamenting the loss of something or an opportunity that you didn't take? Do you always jump to the future? Are you always making plans and creating rules to live by today so that you can have what you want tomorrow? I believe you may be missing out.

When you live in the past you're living with regret. When you live in the future you're living in fear. Surely, it's better to live in the present and enjoy the moment? For some, it can be hard to do that, but if you can learn mindfulness and self-compassion, you'll find it easier.

Mindfulness can stop time because it can slow the mind's tendency to self-judge and self-critique, which we look at in detail in Chapter 4. With this process, you can begin to experience a softening of your heart, a relief from rigidity, hostility and rejection. The next time you're out and about, try and notice the small things around you, such as the colour of the leaves or the feel of the breeze. Access all your senses. If you notice your mind wandering backwards or forwards, mindfully pull it back. It takes practice, but it's worth it!

Learning how to stop your mind from thinking backwards or jumping forwards can be hard if you've been doing it for so long. However, it's something that can have major effects if you dedicate a short amount of time to it every single day. Remember we are working to achieve a life position of 'I'm Okay'.

Exercise 1.3
Mindfulness meditation

This exercise is a short (approximately four-minute) meditation to help you begin on your mindfulness journey.

This meditation offers you the opportunity to start your day with a few minutes of mindfulness, gratitude and loving kindness. Taking the time to do this can go a long way towards creating positive momentum throughout your day. Begin by finding a comfortable position and notice your breath as it comes in and out.

■ Create each breath with your welcoming presence.

■ As you do this, acknowledge the amazing life force within each breath that allows you to be here, right now. Alive, living your life.

■ As you follow your breath in and out, envision your breath carrying oxygen to all parts of your body. To all of your cells, nourishing you. Feel your breath as it spreads throughout your body. Connecting all parts of you, making up the wholeness of who you are.

- See each breath as an invitation to find that place of calmness and stillness within, where you can pause and drop your anchor before you start your day.

- From this inner stillness make space to notice whatever is present within you. Take an inventory accepting wherever you are right now.

- Welcome in this new day! It is yours and you can make of it whatever you want. Each moment today offers a chance for your best self to show up. Each moment offers you a chance to awaken to the here and now.

- Can you find the gifts in this moment? Think of something you are grateful for – large or small. It could be as small as having these few minutes to nurture yourself. Let the feeling of gratitude fill you up.

- Where do you feel more strongly?

- Feel it flowing from head to toe. Let this care and loving kindness spread out into the wider world. Extend feelings of care and compassion to yourself. Appreciate and acknowledge that you have taken this time for you.

■ When you take time for yourself to connect inward and to call up positive feelings within this has a ripple effect that can spread positivity into the lives of those around you.

■ When you are ready, take slow deep breaths bringing your awareness back into the room.

Can you **Stop**, **Reflect** and **Feel** for a moment? Make a list of the nuances of this moment as you read this book. What are you smelling? Can you hear the buzz of the heating, birds or cars outside, the chatter in the background?

_____

_____

_____

_____

_____

_____

_____

Now, check in with your emotions using the emotions list on p. 20. What does it feel like having these moments to check in with yourself?

_____

Did any thoughts arise in connection with the meditation; if so what were they?

_____

Were you able to bring a sense of kindness to your experience?

_____

Through meditation, we can acquire and acknowledge our connection with our authentic self. Meditation can support you to feel grounded where you become aware emotionally and physically via your five senses of the things, people, situations and events around you and simultaneously aware of the physical sensations in your bodies. Can you give yourself five minutes every day to be mindful of where you are, through a short meditation practice?

As you are learning, self-esteem is the overall opinion you have about yourself. I repeat this because I want you to know it's about **you**. To develop self-esteem, a sense of self-worth is required. The opinion you have about yourself can affect what you are prepared to try and not try and a small practice of meditation can go a long way to improving things. If your opinion is negative it can prevent you from reaching your full potential and goals.

If you have a low amount of self-esteem, you might miss that fantastic job opportunity that came your way, simply because you didn't think you were good enough to be selected for the role. The truth is that you are good enough and you probably would have stood a fantastic chance of bagging that job, but you told yourself something different and as a result, chose not to pursue it. These decisions, whether big or small, can alter your life's path and leave you at the end in a state of regret or satisfaction, depending upon which way you choose to go. If you appreciate yourself today, pat yourself on the back. As you progress through this book can you be your biggest cheerleader?

Self-Esteem vs Self-Confidence

Anna is a successful, professional woman who feels confident because she has committed herself to her work. She has been appreciated by her peers because of her remarkable understanding and thrives in her career. At the same time, she lacks self-esteem about her physical looks. She criticises her height, her face and she is depressed and anxious at times. Her professional side always helps her personal side to come out of depression to feel more confident about herself. In other words, her profession becomes her support system to improve her self-esteem in her personal life.

Upon reading this you may think Anna is in an 'I'm okay' position. She is a professional woman who appears okay, however, she is very much 'not okay'. She has confidence in what she does day to day, however, her self-esteem is low.

So, how is self-esteem different from another term we hear a lot, self-confidence?

Self-esteem and self-confidence are very closely linked, and the terms are sometimes used interchangeably, but they are referring to subtly different things. Self-confidence is about the confidence or feelings you have about your ability to do things, not about who you are in general. This shifts and changes depending upon how you're feeling or the situation you're in and whether you've encountered it before, or not.

On the other hand, self-confidence becomes complicated because it can vary from ability to ability. For instance, you may have a high level of self-confidence in your driving skills, because you consider yourself to be a good driver. However, you may have low self-confidence levels when it comes to cooking skills because you've had several cooking disasters.

People with low self-esteem don't believe in their capabilities, they don't see the good in themselves and as a result, lose the confidence to go ahead and fight it out. However, people with increased levels of self-esteem realise their strengths and positives. As a result, they have a level of confidence to make mountains move. It's healthy to build positive self-esteem to create confidence.

Many people consider self-esteem to be a personality trait, something which doesn't alter throughout life, but that's not the case. Remember the continuum on p. 17? Many different situations and environments in life can affect your self-esteem and cause it to tumble.

Individuals can behave in an 'I'm Okay, You're Not Okay', position at home, then head to work and be 'I'm Not Okay, You're Okay' with the boss, then later that evening be 'I'm Okay and You're Okay' with their friends.

Environment

Sometimes when your self-esteem is low it is difficult to see that change is possible. By being able to look at separate areas and environments of your life, this can support you to get more focused on which areas you might want to address. Sometimes, simple interactions in different environments can perpetuate doubt about who you are. For example, taking on responsibilities, dating, interacting with different people, career transitions and health issues can open up many new experiences that shape our self-esteem.

Exercise 1.4

Environment check part 1

Circle the below environments that you feel affect your self-esteem. You may want to add to this list. Once you have circled them, try writing a simple sentence to describe how you think this environment affects you. For example:

Close family – *relationships that bring me down*

Education – *this was a waste of time, I felt judged*

Friendship – *I feel invisible and not myself in some friendship groups*

Close family _____

Extended Family _____

Education _____

Friendships _____

Children _____

Religion _____

Finance _____

Culture_____

Time_____

Leisure_____

Health_____

Career_____

Financial_____

Gerry has been in a loving relationship of ten years and his partner would like to try for a baby. Gerry doesn't feel confident about the idea of being a father because of his own troubled childhood experiences. He feels clumsy and awkward when the topic comes up. He loves children and loves his partner dearly. Gerry feels pressured into achieving unrealistic targets he has placed on himself in being a parent along with trauma from his childhood. Gerry's self-esteem is high in his work life but he experiences anxiety and low esteem in his family life.

This is an example of how our environment can impact how we view ourselves. Someone who is in the grips of depression, anxiety or a very stressful period in their life, will no doubt notice their self-esteem is affected detrimentally. In Gerry's case, he is in a loving relationship, however because of childhood experiences he finds it difficult to consider having children. People with low self-esteem will have little faith in themselves. There will be occasions when it's not possible to be a positive and upbeat person when they are feeling low.

If a person develops depression or anxiety, or they're going through a hard time, it's normal for self-esteem to suffer as a side effect. Depression, anxiety and the like cannot be conquered by boosting self-esteem alone, but it's certainly a very useful concept in the battle overall. The entire condition is based around suppressing a person's spirit, forcing them to see the darkness before the light, and as a result, self-esteem plunges drastically. When your self-esteem is low, you can lose yourself in daydreams, fantasies, memories, plans and fears. Nevertheless, the same can be said for anxiety conditions because self-doubt and lack of trust start to eat away at how you feel.

Part and parcel of dealing with conditions such as these is tackling self-esteem. Let's remember that self-esteem is not a fixed entity:

your level of self-esteem can change and alter according to different experiences and environments. Almost everyone wants to feel good about themselves which is why understanding self-esteem can be appealing and extremely beneficial to your overall happiness in life.

Exercise 1.5

Environment check part 2

How might low self-esteem be connected to your environmental stressors or challenges in your life?

_____

_____

_____

From this exercise, I hope you have been able to **Stop**, **Reflect** and **Feel** how low self-esteem is connected to your environment.

Takeaways

- Mindfulness – or present-moment awareness – is an important and useful skill to cultivate
- Self-esteem and self-confidence are not the same thing
- Your environment affects and plays a huge part in your self-esteem
- You are your biggest cheerleader

2 Understanding Self-Esteem

Self-esteem is not fixed; it can change over time. Healthy self-esteem is being able to hold a realistic and positive image of yourself, one that shows self-acceptance and self-worth, despite the challenges of life's setbacks and pitfalls. Because let's be honest, setbacks and pitfalls are a normal part of life, and of course they can throw you from time to time. Self-esteem isn't about never being challenged, it's about how you ride out those storms and understand that problems are simply a part of life.

Consider the following example:

Amy plays netball, which she enjoys. However, Amy feels she doesn't have a voice around team decisions. She goes along with other people's points of view, even when she doesn't agree with them. This is a common pattern. She finds it hard to speak her truth. She calls herself a loser for not sharing her thoughts and beats herself up for not challenging herself.

Do you recognise aspects of yourself in Amy? Can you relate to someone who finds it hard to speak up? Many of these sorts of feeling often begin in childhood or during adolescence when vulnerability is high; it might seem hard to pinpoint a connection at first, and in some cases, it might be difficult to explore that area, but by doing so you'll reach a greater sense of enlightenment, so be brave enough to open up and stick with the process.

Common Causes of Low Self-Esteem

It's important to remember that everyone is different and that means one size never fits all. Your specific reason for having low self-esteem might not be on the following list, and it could also be that you recognise and can relate to several, which may have joined together to cause a cocktail of negative effects in how you view yourself.

Have you experienced any of the following?

- Unsupportive parents or caregivers in childhood (*see* Anna's story, p. 71)

- Being constantly reminded of your shortcomings by someone in your life, be it a partner, parent, employer or friend (*see* Peter's story, p. 86)

- Bad influences in your teenage years have led towards making poor and damaging decisions (*see* Kate's story, p. 59)

- Stress, such as changing jobs, losing a job, moving house, going through a divorce

- Historical abuse or a traumatic event in your past (*see* Patricia's story, p. 119)

- Grief (*see* Susie's story, p. 139)

- Being pressured into achieving unrealistic targets, in childhood, in the workplace or in the family (*see* Lucia's story, p. 113)

- Mental health conditions such as depression, anxiety, bipolar disorder, post-traumatic stress or obsessive-compulsive disorders (*see* John's story, p. 102)

- Spending too much time alone, feeling isolated and lonely

- Being bullied, either now or in the past (*see* Mo's story, p. 114)

- An extended period of poor health

- Social media anxiety (*see* Dan's story, p. 153)

- Abuse (physical, sexual, emotional) (*see* Robin's story, p. 62)

If you have experienced any of the above, please be sure to take care of yourself as you work on these areas and progress through the book. This book may become the first of many steps towards healing some of your experiences. I encourage you to seek the support of professionals when needed. Please see the resources section on p. 117 to give you some direction as to where you can reach out; doing so will unlock your potential and help you to heal old wounds.

Exploring your family history can sometimes offer insight into the early origins of problems with low self-esteem. Because many challenges around self-esteem can present themselves in here-and-now struggles, it can often be difficult or even impossible to pinpoint exactly where this low self-esteem stems from. Your self-esteem in both childhood and adulthood is impacted by things you experience in external settings.

Many experiences can occur within our friendships and relation-ships as well as in what we view and observe in the world around us. For example, our interactions with our peers, friends, extended family, strangers and teachers can all have an impact on our self-esteem. Many vulnerabilities around our self-esteem can be created from interactions with the people we come across. Overt or even implied criticism or ridicule by any of the above can make anyone question their value and that can drastically affect self-esteem over time.

Comfort, Stretch, Panic

We all sit in our comfort zones from time to time, basically because it's, well, pretty comfortable! We know what's going to happen, we feel safe there, and it's somewhere we aren't going to experience surprises. The problem is, life does start when you dare to stretch your legs just a little outside of that zone.

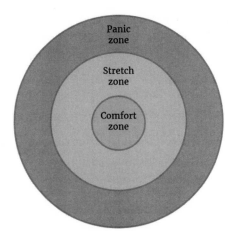

So, I invite you to step out of your comfort zone, the place which is so familiar to you. Often there is no fear or discomfort and you feel very much at home and safe around your choices. Within this zone, there are no challenges or spaces to reflect. Things stay the same and unchallenged.

Exercise 2.1

Discovering your comfort and panic zones

The Comfort Zone

Qualities you experience in your comfort zone, when you are engaged in familiar activities – you're invited to tick the ones that apply to you.

- Calm and at ease

- Complacent

- Comfortable

- Safe

- Gathering your strength

- Recovering

- Low anxiety

- Bored

- Other. . . . .

The Panic Zone

When we consider exploring new ways of being, we often fear the 'panic zone'. This place can feel overwhelming and loaded with stress and fears. It can trigger our flight-or-fight responses. A huge amount of energy is consumed in managing this fear and panic. The thing is, the panic zone is often an illusion because whenever you step outside of your comfort zone, your fears are rarely real.

Qualities you experience in the panic zone; again, please tick the ones that apply to you.

- Scared

- Distressed

- Overwhelmed

- Alert mode

- Fright, flight or freeze reactions

- Overwhelmed

- Stressed

- Fearful

- Anxious

- Loss of focus

- Other. . . . .

The Stretch Zone

The stretch zone is the zone that sits in between. New challenges such as difficult conversations, activities, situations may feel awkward and unfamiliar to you. However, it is in this stretch zone that the magic happens. This is the zone where you can work towards your personal development. You can expand your comfort zone so you can become familiar with new situations, without experiencing the overwhelming panic and worry that would hit you in the face if you simply jumped into the unknown.

This could include:

- Engaging with the new or unknown

- Taking manageable risks

- Challenging yourself but not too much

- Feeling excited and energised

The more you encourage yourself, the more you move from the 'I'm Not Okay' position to the 'I'm Okay' position. Don't you think you owe it to yourself to give it a try? Life can become so much more fulfilling when you step into the stretch zone. There will be more opportunities coming your way as a result. It's surprising just how much your life can change when you commit time and effort to just being brave and giving life a real shot. The opportunities for personal growth and for experiences to live through are truly endless and can only be accessed when you edge your way out of your comfort zone and into the stretch zone.

Exercise 2.2

Stretching your zones

It's time to **Stop**, **Reflect** and **Feel** as you consider these questions. You might want to write the answers down in your journal.

- How much time, roughly speaking, do you spend in each zone each week? How does that feel to you?

- What does your comfort zone look like in different areas (work, home, social relations, health, etc.)?

- How does your body feel when you're in the comfort zone?

- Do you spend too much time in your comfort zone, not enough, or the right amount?

- What does your stretch zone look like in different areas? (Remember your environments, work, home, social relations, health, etc.)?

- What internal voices do you hear when you attempt to move out of your comfort zone into your stretch zone?

Remember you cannot change what you do not acknowledge, so when it comes to your self-esteem, you have to take the time to consider the moments of suffering. Acknowledging this can be difficult for some, but you need to grit your teeth and do your best here. By working through the painful feelings and experiences in your life, my hope is you'll be able to set yourself free from the limitations that you are unknowingly imposing on yourself.

For example, you may have grown up in a culture where you have adopted the 'stiff upper lip' way of thinking. You may have grown up in a society that doesn't favour people who complain, voice their concerns and speak their truth. You might have grown up in a society that was full of expectations, which places pressure on you to achieve certain things by certain times in life.

If you think back over your lifetime, you have met many people, but it's now time to meet yourself and to become your own best friend. When you commit to getting to know yourself by learning a new language, joining that dating app, changing career, addressing your health, being mindful of your friendship groups and recognising what's important to you, then you are on the right track to expand your self-esteem.

Nevertheless, change occurs when you become what you are, not when you try to become what you are not. When you learn to accept your strengths and weakness and tolerate your experiences, your sense of self-esteem starts to transform and change can take place because of this awareness. However, if you try and copy someone else or imitate someone you have seen on TV or in a magazine, growth won't happen because you're trying to get to know someone who truly doesn't exist. So be yourself and recognise your flaws and imperfections.

Strengths & Qualities

The next exercise is about your strengths and qualities. It can be challenging for people with low self-esteem to think of even a single thing that they like about themselves. Of course, they do have positive qualities, it's just they're having difficulty seeing them. This exercise will help you build a positive self-image. Don't be afraid to review regularly and add new qualities. It is an exercise for you to question and evaluate where you are with your self-esteem so you can reflect inwardly and take stock of what makes you you.

Exercise 2.3

What are your strengths and qualities?

Things I am good at:

1

2

3

What I like about my appearance:

1

2

3

I've helped others by:

1

2

3

What I value the most:

1

2

3

Challenges I have overcome:

1

2

3

Times I have made other people happy:

1

2

3

Things that make me unique:

1

2

3

Did you get clarity on your strengths and qualities? I would like you to pay close attention to your reactions to the exercises in this chapter. The more aware you are, the more autonomy you have. Information is power, so anything which comes to you throughout these exercises can be jotted down and used as ammunition for change. Whether you believe it to be good, bad or neither, write it down and reflect on it. You never know how powerful that piece of information could turn out to be.

Exercise 2.4
Journal task

Jot down the experiences from your past that have perhaps held you back from having healthier self-esteem.

Examples:

■ If I had stepped out of my comfort zone when I was in a good relationship I would not have sabotaged my chances of love.

■ If I didn't put myself down so much – which is a family trait – people would take me more seriously.

By now my hope is you are slowly building a picture that will help you to understand your strengths and weaknesses and in turn acknowledge your humanity. These exercises will support you to access your inner voice. Within your inner voice is your belief system and your intuition. It houses all the information about who you are as a person, including your likes, dislikes, your desires, your dreams and everything that makes you you. It also houses your self-esteem, which feeds you the power to go after those things you have always dreamed of. By understanding it, you can make necessary changes that could springboard you towards positive change.

Takeaways

- Consider where your self-esteem may stem from
- Explore your strengths and qualities to heighten your awareness and help correct ineffective behaviours
- Reflect on understanding who you are, what you believe and what you value as an individual

3 Childhood Experiences

So far, we have looked at the significance of making a change concerning your self-esteem. To begin building self-esteem it's important to resist the pressure to conform. If you feel like you are conforming to this process, put the book down, grab yourself a cup of tea and come back to it later. I suggest this because I wonder how often do you listen to family or friends or acquaintances who have no basis for the opinions they are giving you? My hope for you is to encourage you to go through this book because you want to and are ready to make change.

It is important to be open-minded about how much your past experiences affect the here and now. Communication breakdowns with ourselves and others happen because we're not fully present in our feelings, thinking and behaviours. It's best to learn to be firmly in the moment, to stop thinking and moving back to the past, and to avoid jumping into the future. However, this can be a challenge when we experience moments of feeling stuck, lost and disillusioned about who we are.

Many children growing up don't recognise or understand their self-worth and will conform to get their needs met. They will often look to others for permission, which we cover in Chapter 4. With this desire to conform they may be denying their own needs and wants to satisfy the needs of their parents and caregivers.

For example: someone may go into a line of work to please the family rather than pursue their own dreams. Another may feel discouraged to travel to certain holiday destinations because it's not where the family goes. Someone else may shy away from showing they are hurting and another may exhaust themselves in wanting to always get things right. In all of these situations it's easier to go with the needs of others than your own.

Renowned psychologist Carl Rogers describes this as 'conditional positive regard', whereby children only receive positive attention from significant others (such as parents or caregivers) when they behave in a certain way. It's hard to believe that we act in 'certain ways' because we are likely to get a level of recognition; however, this is about surviving. When complying, it reinforces to the child they are only worthy when they behave and act in a certain way. This means that the child is far more likely to act in that way to receive the praise which makes them feel good.

Exercise 3.1
Memory lane

What experiences from your past might have held you back from having healthier self-esteem?

_____

_____

_____

Examples:

- *I gave up my dream of being a dancer because of the messages from family that I wouldn't succeed.*

- *Growing up nobody talked about emotions so today I find it difficult to share my feelings.*

Kate is 28. She has struggled with her weight all her life. She remembers being called 'fat' at school and deciding to not mix with her classmates. She finds it difficult to socialise. Even though her parents appeared supportive, they were often frustrated with her. She believes the 'put-downs' were a way of motivating her to lose weight. Kate told herself she was not good enough. Being constantly reminded of her shortcomings by her family has had an impact on her self-esteem. Kate's foundations for her low self-esteem were laid down early in life. She still hears the messages from her parents that she is not good enough.

From this, we can deduce that Kate has adopted the stance of 'I'm Not Okay'. Children are impressionable, and often learn lessons from what they experience and witness. Children long for respect, acceptance and concern shown by others. Children may internalise every message they encounter as they form a sense of their identity during their early years and into adolescence. Some messages can be interpreted as negative and hurtful, which can in effect harm their self-esteem.

What is coming up for you right now hearing Kate's story? I invite you to **Stop**, **Reflect** and **Feel**. Grab your journal a record what's going on for you. I cover appearances in Chapter 9.

Low self-esteem in children is often related to emotional and physical punishment and withholding of love and affection by parents. As an adult, you understand that all other adults don't have to accept you for you to feel OK about yourself. Children generalise their wellbeing; their level of worth and value are intimately connected. They seek acceptance from *everyone*. Of course, that is unrealistic. The feeling of positive self-esteem is one of the most challenging lessons children learn. However, they learn it to survive.

A handful of negative exposures can often contribute to low self-esteem. For example, if you had a parent who had low self-esteem there is a chance that their behaviour could have been mirrored to you. As a child, you can decide to be that way or choose to ensure you are the complete opposite of that parent.

A nurturing parent conveys thoughts and feelings of love through action. A nurturing parent adopts the 'I'm Okay, You're Okay' stance with their children. However, if a parent is experiencing their own challenges, the child could easily adopt a sense of 'I'm Not Ok and You're Not Okay'. A nurturing parent or caregiver also conveys a sense of worth about their child by providing positive 'Strokes', which we will look at in Chapter 5.

I am aware all of this talk about childhood can be triggering and weighty and I ask that you take a short break. If you can, step outside wherever you are, put the kettle on, or have a nice bath or shower or consider doing the meditation exercise from the previous chapter.

External Influences

Remember the story of the *Wizard of Oz*? Too often many of us act like tin men, scarecrows or frightened lions, expecting others to provide the solutions to our challenges and difficulties. But I believe that the solutions to difficulties are within us all. We have to learn to listen to *ourselves* and not let our voices be drowned out by others'.

Robin experiences low self-esteem resulting from emotional abuse as a child. He feels that he is not particularly good at anything. He has been in the same company for over fifteen years. He has so many other interests but plays it safe. Since his promotion to a senior position, he has felt anxious and he has questioned his purpose and ability to function. He struggles to get up in the morning. He feels unsure about what he wants to do with his life.

Many messages are given to us which can lead to inadequate choices being made, about our thinking, our feelings and our behaviours. We explore powerful messages in detail in Chapter 7.

Powerful messages can show up in the form of the media, family and friendship groups. These messages can lead to chronic impairment of functioning in areas of your life. Without realising it, our influencers can be nurturing or unknowingly neglectful.

A nurturer is someone who gives you a sense of your competency and possibility. There is a difference between being helped and being treated as though you are helpless. Often without realising it, caregivers and parents may interfere with your learning process because they can do something better.

As we've already explored, how we view ourselves outside our immediate network in society can have an impact on how we feel. Do you remember how you responded to the environment exercise in Chapter 1 (p. 34)? We often link and liken our various expectations with value and worth. In an ideal world, it would be easy to develop and maintain healthy self-esteem if we were shielded from external influences, but in reality, that's simply impossible.

Exercise 3.2

External influences

Are you able to share with yourself what stands out more: positive happy stories or negative ones?

_____

_____

_____

Examples:

- My teacher once told me that I would not get a good job, and this has stayed with me for years.

- My aunt once said if I disagree with my husband, I will grow old alone, so I never challenge my husband.

- My best friend in school said my haircut was not ladylike.

We have an innate need to think back to the past. We all do it, but the truth is that we can't go back and change anything that has already happened. Living with regret over anything that has happened in the past is like trying to swim through mud – you can't see clearly and you're achieving nothing.

We are unable to change the past, however through this process of discovery and stretching you can begin to get to know a different version of you and learn from your mistakes.

Can you be realistic about who you are and what you can achieve? Nobody is perfect, and we cannot always have and do it all. However, we can love and accept ourselves the way we are, including our limitations and flaws. Perfection is an illusion, so be easy on yourself. Every single person on this planet has a different view of what perfection is, so trying to achieve it means that you're never going to be happy. Learn to love yourself as you are now, embracing the fact that you're going to change and grow throughout your lifetime. As you work through these exercises you can begin to clarify your childhood perceptions and this in turn can begin to challenge some of your misconceptions.

Exercise 3.3

Who are your nurturers?

List as many as you can remember of the friends and family who nurture you and jot down why they nurture you.

_____

_____

_____

_____

Example: *My mother, she is always encouraging me to go for opportunities.*

List as many as you can remember of the friends or family who have negatively influenced you.

_____

_____

_____

Example: *Uncle Fred, he always said I was lazy and troublesome.*

What was it like doing that exercise? I ask this because it's worth reflecting on whether your past influencers have lived a life that you would want. Perhaps their negative opinions were in fact based on their fears.

Saying No

When was the last time you said no and meant it? When you find it difficult to be assertive it can be tough saying no to other people's requests. Saying no can trigger self-critical thoughts which can lead to feelings of guilt.

To avoid this pain, many people say yes to many requests. Conforming and agreeing to do things that we don't want to do reinforces that our needs and wants are not important. This approach evokes feelings of sadness and low self-esteem. Many of us have been expected to live for other people and to conform to the expectations of grown-ups, to the exclusion of our own needs and wants. Agreeing to do everything can also cause stress because there are only so many hours in the day!

How often do you go along with what others want, because it's easier, only to feel that you have somehow betrayed yourself in the process?

To begin the process of building self-esteem, it's important to challenge the pressure to conform to unrealistic standards. You must be realistic about who you are and what you can achieve. You will form many different narratives around how you view yourself. However, you will also create many fantasies in your mind, both positive and negative, if you start to say no.

The reality is nobody is perfect, and you cannot always have and do it all. However, you can learn to love and accept yourself the way you are, with your limitations and flaws included, so start to say no.

Loving yourself is you taking complete responsibility for yourself. It means taking care of your own emotional needs. It means respecting and valuing yourself, and not depending on anyone else to respect or value you so that you can feel good about yourself.

For example, someone with low self-esteem with their identity and their thinking may tend to over-adapt in their relationships and to be dependent on others. This behaviour occurs when people find it difficult to identify a goal for themselves when attempting to solve a problem. They try to achieve because they believe this to be someone else's goal rather than their own. Sadly, our brains lean more towards negative bias and we may often take on board negative information rather than seeing the positives. Put simply, the human brain is hard-wired to be negative before it is positive, and all of this dates back to the days when cavemen and cavewomen were trying to escape all manner of terrifying threats to survival. Our brains may be hugely sophisticated, but they're still stuck in that survival and threat mode.

I invite you to consider that getting this far into the book means it's time to start putting your own needs first, as well as a time to break out of any programmed parental conditioning that reminds you that making yourself a priority is 'self-centred' or 'selfish'. We have spoken about the importance of awareness and mindfulness and I encourage you to ponder on your automatic decisions to simply do something for someone versus doing what you are want to do.

Allow yourself to **Stop**, **Reflect** and **Feel** before you make decisions. This can give you space to consider if you are *wanting* to say yes as opposed to feeling that pull to respond to the needs of others. If you consider yourself to be a 'nice', 'good', 'reliable' person that many have been able to depend on, it may be a challenge to break this habit. Fears may kick in that others don't like you anymore, which goes back to our brains leaning more towards the negative. This is your inner critic at work which we will get to know in Chapter 4. I encourage you to consider that by truly taking care of yourself out of respect and love for yourself, others are likely to respect and love you more.

Showing Up

Many people with low self-esteem confuse showing up for themselves with showing off. When Maslow wrote about human needs, it is worth noting that he rated 'self-esteem' and the 'esteem of others' on an equal level. One doesn't supersede the other. Nor does one flow from the other.

A sense of esteem from others can trigger your own sense of self-esteem. This ties into the childhood experiences, and so I encourage you to **Stop**, **Reflect** and **Feel** what was mirrored to you by your caregivers as a child. As you know, parental influences may very well plant the seed of low self-esteem, which unknowingly can guide you to choose a path that may lead to limiting growth.

Everything you experience can have an impact on your self-esteem, whether negatively or positively. As you move through childhood, adolescence and adulthood, you receive messages about what is considered right or wrong, acceptable and desirable, good or bad, a success or a failure. You make comparisons questioning whether your own identity is enough. In essence, you are assessing whether your achievements, your needs and your wants fit into the moulds of others'. If they do, you feel good; if they don't, you feel like you need to change. Having this awareness of your process can bring about change.

Anna was acceptable in her family only when she was receiving good grades and listening to her parents' instructions. According to her grandmother and mother, she was not beautiful because she did not meet their criteria of beauty. However, her sister was extremely beautiful and received most of their praise. To gain her parents' and grandparents' attention, Anna diverted her efforts towards studies and tried to get good results. Exam results days were the only moments when she felt appreciated and accepted. All those positive conditional regards made her an obedient and compliant child whose responsibility was to please her parents. These influences in her teenage years have led her towards her having low self-esteem. In this process, she lost her original self and her self-esteem became dependent on positive affirmations from her educational surroundings.

Can you relate to parts of Anna's story? One of the biggest challenges for people building self-esteem is navigating the constant barrage of expectations and stereotypes conveyed by our society, and there are many. Consequently, external expectations can create impossible standards, social pressures and traits of perfectionism. All this is covered in Chapter 9's section on social media. When all these come together they can create an environment that makes it very challenging for people to feel adequate and worthy.

Luckily a shift can take place when you become more aware of how you are the expectations affect you. By separating yourself from negative messages that may hinder you and tarnish your self-image you can become more realistic about what you expect of yourself and disregard the expectations of others.

Exercise 3.4

About me

Growing up I felt _____

My parents or caregivers were _____

My relationships with siblings were_____

Best aspects of my childhood were _____

Worst parts of my childhood were_____

Browse over your responses and consider if any of them appear to be factors that have played a role in hindering healthy self-esteem. The exercises are created for you to know yourself, be yourself and own yourself. Grab your journal and write down what is coming up for you.

Exercise 3.5
Milestones

Can you **Stop**, **Reflect** and **Feel**, then record the so-called milestones you placed on yourself growing up? e.g. By a certain age you wanted to...

_____

_____

_____

Example: By age 30 I want to be married.

This is a good way to bring home the sheer number of expectations that are placed upon you every single day. By not meeting one of those so-called milestones, you may feel like you're failing. Can you be kind to yourself and consider life is not a race and you have to live at your own pace?

Expectations aren't real, they don't make you happier, they're not set in stone and they're assumptions of the way things should be

- who makes these rules? Who decides how you should be or how you should act? What is key in addressing your self-esteem is believing in yourself and embracing ALL that you are. The truth of the matter is that every single thing you are seeking externally needs to be addressed and resolved internally first.

Takeaways
- Consider how much historical childhood experiences and external influences can impact your self-esteem
- Explore how you show up today in the here and now, and how that supports your levels of self esteem
- Reflect on milestones that have been created by you or others and if they have had an impact on your self-esteem

4 The Power of the Inner Critic

Have you experienced your inner critic?

Believe it or not, the inner critic that is a part of you and keeps trying to get your attention is actually concerned about your well-being. Many researchers will say it's attempting to care for you – but in a painful and unhelpful way

I encourage you as a reader to get to know your inner critic and to consider acknowledging its intentions. We don't want to *condone* its harsh approach to your thinking, we just want to create the space that will allow you to explore the feelings and needs that it's trying to express. The inner critic can leave you feeling 'I'm Not Okay, You're Okay' and 'I'm Not Okay and You're Not Okay'. When it pipes up, you might feel shame, frustration, hopelessness, sadness, self-doubt, fear or irritability.

How often have you heard yourself saying the following?

- I don't deserve this
- I'm such an idiot
- It's always my fault
- I can't do anything right
- What is wrong with me?
- I don't deserve this success
- I don't belong
- I am not smart enough
- I just got lucky
- I can't believe they trusted me
- I am not good enough to do this
- I don't deserve this job

The inner critic may be the voice of your parents, peers or teachers, or siblings from many years ago. It also might be indirect, where your influencers and significant others didn't tell you outright that you were stupid, overweight, not good enough, not important or unlovable. Many people want to banish their inner critic for good, especially when they are first aware of it and how much pain the inner critic is bringing to a situation. However, it's not possible to ignore it, tell it to shut up or push it away somehow, because of it's part of your internal programming. So, we need to consciously give ourselves permission to change.

Exercise 4.1

Minute test

Try and jot down three of your positive qualities in under a minute.

_____

_____

_____

_____

_____

_____

How easy was it to do? At the end of this book my hope is that you will have no trouble recalling positive things about yourself. You might have found it challenging to do at first, and may have written very little.

Many people struggle to think of things on the spot, and this is because when you have low self-esteem you may lean towards the negative things that may confirm your negative view of yourself. If you didn't manage to jot down some positive qualities about yourself in under a minute, this is an area that needs working on. Acting spontaneously requires you to have confidence in your abilities and the freedom to express yourself.

Get to Know Your Inner Critic

Sometimes, it's hard to identify the inner critic among the chatter in your head, but your feelings can serve as clues that the inner critic is present. Many messages we receive and internalise in childhood can become a part of our view of ourselves and we can't differentiate them as critical. These messages can contribute to the tone of our inner voice or inner critic.

Everyone has an inner critic and some are crueller than others. The inner critic criticises you, compares you to others and fills you with self-doubt. And ultimately it prevents you from living from a place of unconditional love. The inner critic has a purpose, and once you learn more about the inner critic you can engage with it. Let's remember it was developed through your childhood experiences and now you are getting to know it.

Mikey feels self-conscious when he is socialising. He's convinced people are judging him and looking at him. He tells himself people think he's ugly or weird because of the size of his ears. He dislikes going into a room full of people. He is so aware of his discomfort that he comes out in a sweat and tenses up. He fears everyone notices this.

Can you relate to any of Mikey's experiences? His inner critic is harsh and unrelenting. Mikey hears he is not good enough, he is not smart enough and he is unworthy. His negative self-judgements contribute to his low self-esteem and keep him in the position of 'I'm Not Okay'.

The inner critic has many faces and so it might sometimes be subtle: encouraging you to produce better work, do better or show up better. Or it might be an aggressive or abusive voice telling you that you are wrong, bad or seriously flawed. For some people, the inner critic serves the role of keeping them safe from humiliation, failure and threat. With low self-esteem, you can fall into the habit of engaging in negative self-talk, which includes irrational and distorted thinking. This is your inner critic in action.

Low self-esteem can stop you from seeing situations objectively. Your inner critic may be located in the subconscious and it can be looking out for you. Often a subconscious inner critic can turn a situation into self-sabotage. Without even knowing it you may be surrounding yourself with people who only reinforce your inner critic. This will affect your self-esteem every time you're around them, or whenever you communicate with them. Your inner critic can rattle on 24/7 to get your attention on a subconscious and conscious level and it will challenge some of your strongest beliefs about yourself.

For example, if you have an unforgiving inner critic there is a chance you may have directly or indirectly been told negative things about yourself like Mikey. A child that has been abandoned may develop a tough inner critic. The message they hear is 'there must be something wrong with me' and their life position is 'I'm not Okay'.

Exercise 4.2

Inner critic narrative

What kind of critical words or comments did you hear from your immediate external environment e.g. your family, friends, school, etc., which have now become part of how you view of yourself?

Example: *Why didn't you get all As in your GCSE's?*

Boys don't cry.

_____

_____

_____

_____

Let's **Stop**, **Reflect** and **Feel** because it's not easy to see your inner critic narrative on paper. What emotions from Chapter 1 are present with you? If the emotions that arise are powerful, **Stop**, **Reflect** and **Feel**. You may feel helpless to turn your emotions around, however, it's important to give yourself self-compassion and permission to acknowledge them. Can you call upon the nurturer you identified in the previous chapter to positively support you to change the narrative?

The inner critic that lives within you might be subtle and even unknown to you, yet it still exerts its power and dictates the actions you take. It may not be your kindest companion, however its intentions when you are aware of its role can be inherently positive.

Let's remember that negative talk can often start as an external influence that is forced on us by powerful people in our childhood. As children, the voice is internalised and it may help us to survive. However, the reality is that as we get older it can hold us back, and this can cost us our self-esteem and belief in ourselves, diminishing our ability to live happy and fulfilled lives. At some point, you will look back and realise that you spent your life trying to please others, conform to others, show up for others, listen to others and have your entire mindset affected by things that were simply a distorted view of reality. It's not an ideal way to live, and it's certainly not a fulfilling way to live, that's for sure.

We will use these positive traits in Chapter 7 when we reframe your narrative.

Takeaways
- Consider the role your inner critic plays in helping or hindering your self-esteem
- Explore the permissions you give and don't give yourself
- Reflect on your positive traits and shout them out out loud

Part 2

How Authentic Are You?

In this part of the book, we are going to learn more about your authentic self. You will familiarise yourself with who you are.

- Do you believe that you are sometimes not yourself?

- Do you hide certain parts of yourself that you assume to be negative or less than able?

- Do you show a different side of yourself to other people?

If you have answered 'Yes' to any of these questions, you may have challenges in being authentic with yourself.

5 Being You

The word 'authenticity' can evoke many images of something being pure or unadulterated. The act of authenticating is a process of determining that something is indeed genuine. So where are you with your authenticity? If you have challenges with your self-esteem, soak up false flattery, regularly people-please or find yourself always using diplomacy, silence and avoidance, you may be using these coping mechanisms to conceal your authentic self.

Being a people-pleaser, super-compliant or avoiding confrontation betrays your own authenticity. When you're not able to be yourself you constrain your growth and self-esteem.

Carl Rogers developed a form of psychotherapy based on the idea that when people feel truly accepted for who they are, they don't need to put on a mask. So, instead of pretending to themselves or others that they are something they are not, they begin to listen to their own inner voice and begin to make more authentic decisions about how they lead their lives. By being authentic your life can take on new direction, meaning and purpose.

If your self-esteem is challenged you may disguise or manipulate features of your personality to better ensure others are not judgmental towards you. If you worry about what others think of you, then you may manipulate your personality and communication styles to seek approval or avoid disapproval. My hope through this process is you begin to know yourself, own yourself and be yourself.

Many people act differently to their authentic self because being themselves can sometimes be scary. By doing this, they fear opening themselves up to judgement. They fear exposing themselves to the possibility of hurt and heartbreak. The truth is that without doing this in the first place, they are blocking their chances of connecting not only with others, but also, and most importantly, with themselves.

Can you work towards owning your own authenticity?

Exercise 5.1

Explore your authentic self

Grab pen and paper and do a little exploration. The purpose of this exercise is to encourage you to go a little deeper. You cannot understand more about yourself and learn to embrace your authentic self unless you know what you're dealing with from the get-go.

On a scale of 1 to 10, with 1 being poor and 10 being excellent:

- How do you rate yourself in terms of your authenticity?

- Are you your true self around other people, or do you hide or change yourself at all?

- Do you change yourself around certain people? Can you identify who those people are?

- Are these people in authority? Are they people you admire and you're scared of making a fool of yourself in front of?

Now, rate yourself on the same scale and ask yourself these very important questions:

- Do you like who you are when you're around these people?

- Do you feel better than your authentic self, or worse?

What was it like answering those questions? I am curious to know which life position you find yourself in when you reflect back. By getting to know yourself on a deeper level and working towards being authentic, feeling happy in your own skin and having no problems showing the world who you truly are, you're unlocking the door to happiness. When you are free to be yourself, everything in your life changes for the better.

Stroke Theory

Imagine a person sits next to you on the tube and tells you how nice you look today. What effect will this have on you? Will you see it as a positive or negative? For some, it may lift their spirits a bit.

Now imagine, when you arrive at your job, your manager is waiting for you to discuss a meeting. As you rushed out, you forgot your notes for the meeting. Can you imagine how this might affect your inner dialogue or the interactions you have with your boss who doesn't appear pleased? Can you imagine how much your inner critic steps in?

The above examples are personal interactions and in Transactional Analysis Theory, these interactions are called transactions, from one person to another.

As humans, we have many pangs of hunger, and one of them is the need for emotional stimulation, especially in social interactions. If there is a lack of positive stimulation this can affect someone's self-esteem. Many people belittle their achievements and accomplishments. In doing this they are restricting an important source of recognition of who they are. They find it difficult to accept praise and they find it difficult to give themselves positive recognition or, in transactional analysis, positive 'strokes'.

A 'stroke' is defined by US psychotherapist Claude Steiner as a 'unit of recognition'. It can be given by others, like the positive example from one tube passenger to another or the negative example from the line manager.

You can also apply strokes to yourself using your words, language, actions, thoughts and behaviours. Stroking is the vehicle by which you can convey, or not convey, respect, acceptance and concern. People with low self-esteem will often be stroke-deprived.

Giver of Strokes

You may be someone who gives lots of positive strokes and receives very little in return. However, you may have been in the company of people who give out lots of praise and recognition but there are conditions attached to them. My hope through this book is that you can begin to apply strokes to yourself, which means accessing your inner nurturer and feeling much happier in yourself as a result.

Family dynamics, internal and external influences will all play a part in how many positive strokes were experienced during your formative years. The fact you have purchased this book tells me you are allowing yourself to put yourself first because you are deserving. Well done! This is my positive stroke for you. It's a great first step towards a far happier and more fulfilling future.

Remember your inner critic, which not only attacks our self-esteem but also the self-esteem of the people around you? You can give strokes and ask for strokes. You can gladly accept strokes you want and politely reject strokes you don't want. It's all about practice, but the more you develop your self-esteem, the easier it will be to do this without thinking about it.

For some, being amicable and having the ability to have successful relationships with people and blend in with groups can be very important. However, it can be detrimental to your emotional health if you go too far in your efforts to gain social acceptance and positive strokes. In this circumstance, you can lose your authenticity, your voice and instead live and behave in a manner where you prioritise pleasing others and sacrifice being true to yourself. In this case, you're changing your behaviour and yourself to suit other people, perhaps taking on a role which isn't yours naturally, and therefore becoming an entirely different person, a more inauthentic person.

There are three different kinds of strokes:

- Verbal or non-verbal

- Positive or negative

- Conditional or unconditional

Most interactions and conversations are an exchange of strokes. Many will involve both verbal and non-verbal kinds. A positive stroke is one in which the received experiences are pleasant; a negative stroke is one experienced as uncomfortable or painful. People with low self-esteem may satisfy their hunger for strokes by accepting negative behaviour but giving positive strokes in abundance to other people. Do you do this?

There are many other ways you can give yourself strokes. Maybe you take time out to relax in a warm bath with your favourite music or treat yourself to a special meal or trip away. It's important that you don't regard these as rewards for anything, and that you give them to yourself for your own sake, as a way to look after yourself and work with a little self-care.

We will always experience positive and negative strokes, however, the awareness of what you accept and tolerate will be a useful way of learning about your self-esteem. Some strokes may be disguised as positive but actually have a negative connotation. For example, if someone points out you have a nice shirt but in such a way as to make you suspect they're not being genuine.

Self-esteem may consequently be enhanced or weakened by a person's ability to deal with negative messages. For example, a conditional stroke might be when someone tells you they don't like their favourite brew in this way, but they give you the option to make the tea differently. Positive conditional strokes can support competency and growth and they help create a practice of taking responsibility for your own choices, actions and, ultimately, your own self-esteem.

Different Strokes for Different Folks

John experienced anxiety and for years had a pattern of going into relationships with women who eventually abandoned him. He believed that he was seeking positive strokes from the women in his relationships but always ended up feeling either rejected or abandoned. He mostly fell in love with women who did not want to commit to relationships. However, he did not find women who were keen and looking for commitment so attractive. He told himself that every woman would abandon him – like his mother. Later on, he realised that unconsciously he was choosing women who did not meet his needs and wants. John's lack of healthy self-esteem led to him making poor choices.

Can you relate to parts of John's story? Do you accept the behaviours of others that don't serve you? How much have your childhood experiences shaped what you are willing to tolerate? John, like many people, was strokes-deprived as a child and he sought out what was familiar to him. As humans, we crave both negative and positive strokes. We grow and thrive when we get positive strokes and feel defensive and hurt when we get negative ones. Many people dislike it when they don't get any strokes at all. As with so many things in life, our upbringing shapes what strokes are familiar to us. If we grew up with a load of negative strokes, chances are we will seek them and give them out. A genuine compliment, a pleasant phone call from a friend and a pat on the back are all positive strokes.

The next exercise is one which many of my clients find useful because the practice of recording your successes and progresses supports you to appreciate your wins, and this can boost self-esteem. This boost can be leveraged to support you to step out of your comfort zone.

Exercise 5.2

Successes to date

They can be anything, but they need to mean something to you. It can be learning how to cook, moving house and arranging it on your own, learning how to overcome a fear or control your emotions, birthing your first child, gaining a promotion at work, finishing your studies. It can be anything as long as in your eyes it's a 'success'. We often think about success in promotion terms, monetary terms, meeting large milestones in life that we're 'supposed' to achieve, but a success can be anything that you deem to be one. If you feel that learning Japanese was one of your biggest successes, that's great, and something to celebrate. If you feel that learning how to make the perfect pastry was a success to you, well done!

_____

_____

_____

_____

_____

_____

_____

_____

_____

_____

_____

_____

_____

_____

The next exercise is experiential and you may need to phone a
friend. It will enable you to experience and understand your
strengths in positive ways and to be able to receive positive
strokes, to develop a positive sense of worth.

Exercise 5.3
Phone a friend

With a friend, write down a list of ten good things about yourself.

Example: *Good listener, shoulder to cry on*

_____

_____

_____

_____

_____

_____

_____

_____

_____

_____

This exercise can also be done with a group of trusted friends, in which you all take it in turns to brag. The listeners are encouraged to give positive strokes by saying, 'Yes! Great stuff! Well done! Tell us more!'

Please note it is okay to brag openly and sincerely, as this is an exercise for you. By choosing to disrupt and to think differently you can make changes in how you view yourself.

When you have completed this exercise **Stop**, **Reflect** and **Feel**, and grab your journal to record some of the emotions that come up for you. By writing down your wins, successes and achievements you become more aware of your progress.

Takeaways
- Consider the skill of positive stroking as a direct way of building the self-esteem muscle
- Explore how authentic you are day to day
- Reflect on your successes, achievements and accomplishments

6 Boundaries

So far, we have explored what is like to be more authentic with yourself. We have established whether you accept praise and how much your childhood and environment play a part in how you see yourself. By now we know self-esteem development is influenced by two sources; the first from the outside and the second from within.

Do you often give as much of yourself to others as you can, for the sake of giving? If the answer is 'Yes,' then you are not alone. Instead of strengthening our relationships, our 'giving' can at times cause strain. We can find ourselves in a one-sided relationship with a 'taker'. This is a challenge that many people with low self-esteem experience when dealing with their families, peers and friends

Many of our beliefs around how we view ourselves will have roots in our upbringing. Some roots have been more beneficial than others.

- Are you someone who is always doing things for others and never has time for themselves?
- Do your friends always lean on you for advice?

You might feel a sense of pleasure when that happens because you like to help your friends, but if it's happening all the time you have to question whether your boundaries are being respected.

When it comes to addressing your self-esteem, I encourage you to be your own best friend and your best cheerleader. That's right, the same way you are available to a friend in need, to help them feel worthwhile and accepting towards themselves, this behaviour has to come from within you too. By focusing on yourself, you can give yourself permission to think, feel and behave in ways you did not experience when you were young. Boundaries are the limits and rules you set for yourself within relationships. A person with healthy boundaries can say no to others when they want to. However, they are also comfortable opening themselves up to intimacy and close relationships.

Most of us tend to give positivity and affection to others, but we don't give it back to ourselves. For instance, if you give advice to a friend about how to deal with a painful break-up, you probably tell her that she's too good for him; that she needs to take time out and learn to love herself again; that she's wonderful and doesn't deserve the pain. However, if you're going through the same situation, you probably don't tell yourself those things. You probably tell yourself that it was your fault, that you deserve it, that you need to do something to change the situation. We are not the same with ourselves as we are with other people and that needs to change!

Exercise 6.1

Where are your boundaries?

Imagine yourself as a garden. Surrounding that garden there is a fence.

- How high is your fence?

- Does the fence appear secure or is it a bit wobbly?

- Is there a gate you can open?

- Does it have gaps or holes?

- Or has the wind taken it down and it's just hanging?

Only you know what your garden looks like, and only you can take control of what you allow in and allow out. For example: you may have healthy boundaries in your workplace, wobbly boundaries in your relationships and stiff boundaries in your family dynamics. In Chapter 1 we spoke about the environment and how it can have an impact on your self-esteem.

Exercise 6.2
Protect your boundaries

Can you identify in which environments you believe a boundary needs to be firmer to support your self-esteem? This could be in any of the environments we have covered

_____

_____

_____

Example: *I feel obligated to pick up my phone even when I am tired.*

Weak boundaries that have been mirrored and passed on can leave many people vulnerable to low self-esteem. If your gate is permanently open there is a chance others may take you for granted or even cause harm. Of course, this might not be done intentionally, but the effects are still damaging and exactly the same.

- What were boundaries like in your family?

- How often did people take healthy risks?

Healthy self-esteem will produce secure boundaries, ones that show you deserve to be treated well, along with how much you value yourself. Solid boundaries are a measure of healthy self-esteem.

Lucia has decided to speak to her sister about helping in her cafe during the weekends. She enjoys helping out, however it's cutting into her own family time. She is happy to support but not every weekend. Lucia has been finding it difficult to speak up and be honest about the impact the overtime is having on her own life.

Is this you? Do you find it difficult to speak up? She put her sister's needs and wants before her own, so her boundaries were full of holes. Lucia's life position was 'I'm not Okay'.

We have established that ineffective parenting can contribute and results in people placing a low value on themselves and their right to happiness. Another significant reason for defining strong boundaries is remembering the importance of saying 'No' to unreasonable requests, which we covered in Chapter 3. Even the reasonable ones from time to time can conflict with plans.

It is important we take better care of ourselves and not let others define who we are, or manage our time and our expectations, let alone manage our minds. If you are lonely you may widen your boundaries and seek out others for contact, allowing you to spend time with those who make you feel good. If you need time out you may bring your boundaries in closer, by not responding to a call.

Mo works with someone who makes religious jokes which he dislikes. He dreads being around this colleague and feels it's having an impact on his emotional wellbeing.

Mo's boundaries have clearly been crossed and his life position is 'I'm not Okay'. Many workplaces are rife with resentment, bitterness and conflicts that are rarely expressed. Living inauthentically and without boundaries can create tension and distress and this can take an emotional toll. It takes courage to face up to ourselves and humility to accept what we learn, and discipline to take positive action.

This is why boundaries are important; they help us to live in tune with our desires, needs and feelings. They help us to become less concerned about how we are viewed and more satisfied with the perceptions we have about ourselves. Knowing yourself and being mindful of your boundaries is an important part of human interactions.

Can you remind yourself of your self-worth and what matters to you so that no one crosses your boundaries? Grab your journal and write down what is coming up for you. You may want to consider the following questions when you are writing.

- Who in the past has crossed your boundaries?

- How does it make you feel?

- What steps can you take to ensure your boundaries are secure?

Like Mo, if you often feel uncomfortable by how you have been treated, then it could be time to reset your boundaries to a more secure level. Having a clearly defined boundary allows you to take control of your life, and developing healthy self-esteem will produce boundaries that show you deserve to be treated well.

If everyone else is constantly taking up your time, you won't have the opportunity to simply 'be'. Never underestimate the power of just being and spending time with yourself. When others are taking advantage of your kind nature, like in the example of Mo, you are left feeling depleted and lacking in energy. That's not a great recipe for healthy self-esteem. Set your boundaries and stick to them. If you need to let others know about your new boundaries in place, do that also. It's nothing to be ashamed of and it's something to encourage others around you to do too. The healthier boundaries we have, the happier and healthier we can be.

Improving your self-esteem is a long-term goal because it takes practice and effort over time. Well done for getting this far in the book! You may well face setbacks and have bad days, especially when it comes to being honest with yourself. The questions have been designed for you to reflect and have an awareness.

Can you try to accept any setbacks as normal and learn from them to keep you moving forward?

Takeaways
- Consider your boundaries and how you hold them with yourself and others
- Explore where your boundaries start and end
- Reflect on how loose or rigid boundaries may have impacted your self-esteem

7 Powerful Messages

Many people lose their identity as a person in their own right. The good news is that the more you work on yourself, the healthier your self-esteem can be. It's a cumulative effect, a little like a snowball rolling down a hill – the more it builds, the more momentum it picks up and before you know it, there's a huge ball of snow careening down a hill!

Many people who have not learnt to love and accept themselves often play small. As we have learnt, the inner critic can feed them lies and tell them they are not good enough.

Patricia has been through a break-up with an emotionally abusive partner. Her confidence has been eroded to the point where she simply does not know what she believes anymore. Her level of self-esteem is at rock bottom, and because she had been the victim of gaslighting she no longer understands her thoughts either. She feels the pull to return to the abusive ex-partner because it is all she knows. She does not have the confidence to break away and look for a new experience and she lacks the right level of energy and self-worth to say, 'You know what, I don't deserve this, I deserve better.'

Many people are taught to avoid conflict. This can crush self-esteem and allow resentment to build up. When you find the courage to own your truth you can begin to improve the quality of your self-esteem. If you don't believe in yourself how do you expect others to believe in you?

The words 'should' and 'try' are often used subconsciously in our everyday language and they're not always positive for self-esteem. These words can have a big impact on the way we think about ourselves. They are not great motivators. They take you out of the present moment. They strain relationships. They ignore accomplishments and increase negative emotions.

Grab your journal and write down what is coming up for you when you hear the words 'should' and 'try'.

- Are they nurturing you or hindering you?
- How often does your inner critic use these words in any given day?

Example: I hear the 'should' every time I am with my family and it's exhausting.

Behind the words 'should' and 'try' there may be a greater purpose that you are wanting for yourself. However, these words persist and exist in our inner critic because they can often be part of someone else's needs and wants or a societal pressure to be a certain way. Words such as 'could' or 'would' are more encouraging. So rather than, 'You should take out the bins,' consider replacing it with 'You could take out the bins.' Can you give yourself permission to find a way of reframing the 'should' and 'try' that are part of your inner dialogue?

Reframing

Many therapists support clients to focus on positive thinking and replace negative thoughts with positive ones – a strategy called reframing. This is a strategy often used to support people to consider their thoughts, feelings and behaviours from a different perspective. By now you will have pages and pages of thoughts and emotions which you have collected throughout this book.

You must begin to reframe the way you view yourself. As you build your awareness you build your self-esteem, and this in turn increases your insights. Working on your self-esteem is very much like a muscle, it needs to be worked on and the more you work on it, the stronger it becomes. Start flexing that self-esteem!

It's impossible to have high self-esteem if your negative mind is firmly in control. Reframing is a CBT (Cognitive Behavioural Therapy) technique which involves recognising a negative thought and reframing it into something positive, and then repeating it until it becomes second nature. This technique takes time because you need to be aware of your negative thoughts as they enter your mind, but it's a very successful one. The first step to change your automatic thoughts is to notice the themes and emotional tone of your narrative.

Give it a try. The next time you realise you're thinking something negative, perhaps:

'I look fat' try changing that in your mind to 'I love my curves' and then repeat it over and over (aloud if possible).

Or maybe:

'I'm not strong enough' could become 'I am strong, powerful and wonderful' or, 'I am continually learning and growing,' or even, 'I am steadily becoming better.'

Please note, the first option may feel like too much for some, particularly if you're at the beginning of your journey to improve your self-esteem. But others may be at the stage where they truly believe themselves to be the strong, powerful and wonderful person they are. These are tried and tested techniques I have used in the therapy room. Reframing is about the conversations you are having with yourself. Part of the reframing is getting you more into the grey area. Do you remember the continuum of self-esteem? Part of moving towards the middle is being open to the new narrative of how you view yourself.

Now, go back to your affirmations as a way to support your self-esteem (see p. 106). If you feel very conflicted about who you think you are, perhaps reframing some of those limiting beliefs can get you the middle. Don't be afraid to make any adjustments you need so that it sits better with you and leads towards progress.

Adjusting how you experience yourself is always a work in progress, and self-esteem building is about being realistic with yourself versus an overall desire to be perfect, please others or be strong. All reframing has to sit well with you. The more you reframe your negative thoughts, the stronger the positive becomes. In the end, the positive thought always wins over the negative.

The Past, Present & Future

Exercise 7.1

Your life story

I want you to write your life story. This exercise is a popular one because it allows you to **Stop**, **Reflect** and **Feel**. Giving the past, present and future a narrative serves different psychological functions. On the one hand it can strengthen your sense of self, giving you a feeling of continuity from your childhood experiences to the present. On the other hand it can also offer support as you give yourself permission to distance yourself from the negative messages and events of the past. Remember your vision: how you want to exist outside of your comfort zone.

I invite you to write a life story in three parts: the past, present and future. Identify your life position in all three. One gentle reminder, when you live in the past you're living with regret. When you live in the future you're living in fear. I am certain by now you can see the benefits of living in the present.

Your life story can support you to develop a sense of meaning which contributes to fulfilment. Give yourself permission to be creative and I encourage you to think of your personal strengths. When writing about your past, have some compassion as you may be unlocking some difficult memories. When you get to the future section, jot down what your ideal future might look like and how you hope to achieve it.

The Past

Write the story of your past. Be sure to describe challenges you have overcome, and the personal strengths that allowed you to do so. Can you be compassionate towards your past story?

The Present

Describe your life and who you are now. How do you differ from your past self? What are your strengths now? What challenges are you facing?

The Future

Write about your ideal future. How will your life be different than it is now? How will you be different than you are now?

Celebrating You

Nobody likes to highlight their good points, and we're far more adept at highlighting our downsides. This challenge will be linked to your childhood experiences about giving oneself praise, which many people struggle to do. Remembering we are working towards the 'I'm Okay, You're Okay' position. If you're constantly telling everyone about your bad features and qualities, they're going to believe them and not see the good ones.

It's time to celebrate yourself and the wonderful being that you truly are.

Exercise 7.2

How much do you like yourself?

Grab a piece of paper and a pen, sit down somewhere quiet, switch off your phone and again write a list of five things you like about yourself. It has to be five, it can't be any less. Remember you are your biggest cheerleader.

Each day for seven days add one more thing to that list.

Example: *I like my sense of humour.*

_____

_____

_____

_____

_____

Most people struggle to do this because many are encouraged to be humble. Why not celebrate your plus points?

Unhealthy Beliefs

Let's see where you are now on the back of celebrating your plus points. One way of knowing how well you are doing with your self-esteem is your ability to challenge some of those unhealthy beliefs. The next exercise is designed to combat those self-defeating beliefs that you adopted. It is very difficult to counteract beliefs that have become ingrained due to negative experiences or fears. This can be a challenge. I'm giving you a huge round of applause right now for trying to overcome the insecurities you feel as a result of those beliefs.

Everyone has a strong need to survive and survival includes the survival of your inner critic. Be compassionate towards yourself as you go through the following statements and exercises:

Exercise 7.3
Limiting beliefs

Limiting belief: *No one accepts me.*

How real is this statement?

Example: *The rejections from members of my family tells me it's real.*

_____

_____

Let's think of the reframing . . . who does accept you?

Example: *My friends accept me. I realise today they are more like my family.*

_____

_____

The truth: Some people accept you, but do not necessarily show it. Other people can learn to accept you if you show them they are significant, then they feel good about themselves. Some people look as if they do not accept you, but this may not be true. Others may never accept you no matter what you do.

The acceptance and approval of others can change like the weather. This indicates that striving for acceptance and approval can change. For some it can become a useless feat. The search for approval can be personally and emotionally damaging to you and your self-esteem.

I hope that you were able to give yourself a positive stroke in the first belief. It's healthier when we accept and love ourselves, as well as accept into our lives only those who will accept and value us as we are. If a relationship with another person or people is genuine, you will be accepted as you are. If the person expects to benefit from you or satisfy their inner insecurities through you, then the relationship is not and will never be real.

When you learn to let go of people who do not accept you and when you can reject conditional love, you will see how your self-esteem will improve.

Your self-esteem will not improve only because you have eliminated negative influences in your life, but because you love yourself enough to know that you deserve so much more.

Exercise 7.4

More limiting beliefs

Limiting belief: I am incapable.

How real is this statement that you are incapable?

Example: It's real because I have struggled to make it as a successful actress.

_____

_____

Let's reframe... can you make a list of what you *are* capable of doing?

Example: I have other qualities besides acting that I can share with others.

_____

_____

The truth: Is everyone else capable of everything they do? If you think so, banish that thought. No one can do all things capably. You *are* capable. Perhaps you cannot design a bridge or run a charity fund, but you do have your unique capabilities. Remember the successes you listed? You developed your capabilities over the years and used them to demonstrate them in your behaviour.

Limiting belief: *I am afraid of what others think.*

How real is this statement that you must be afraid of what others think?

Example: *For years, I have feared what others think of me.*

_____

_____

Let's reframe... what are the benefits of being afraid of what others think?

Example: *No benefits, I realise now I fear myself more than others. It's all been in my head.*

_____

_____

The truth: No matter what you do, you cannot control the thoughts of another. Socrates said, 'Be true to your own self.' You cannot hope to spend your life pleasing others. There is no use trying to do that. Many people with low self-esteem are the world's biggest people-pleasers.

Limiting belief: Everyone is better and smarter than I am.

How real is this statement that everyone is better and smarter than you?

Example: I compare myself to others who I believe are smarter.

_____

_____

Let's reframe... what you are smart at?

Example: I am just as smart as the next person. I don't need to compare myself as it doesn't serve me because I have my own qualities.

_____

_____

The truth: Everyone is *not* smarter or better than you. This is an irrational belief. If you are in an unfamiliar or uncomfortable situation, you may feel that others are better or smarter. However, the truth is that they are more familiar with it. In time, you too can become more familiar with the environment in which you find yourself. Give yourself a chance and remember that your awareness of you is the start of you getting to know yourself. Can you remember times when you struggled with a situation and then over time you finally got the hang of it, e.g. a previous job, starting new friendships, joining a social group?

Limiting belief: *I don't deserve to be treated with respect.*

How real is this statement that you don't deserve to be respected?

Example: *Many people have disrespected me over the years.*

_____

_____

Let's reframe . . . who in your friendship groups and family respects you?

Example: *I have friends who respect me, so I don't need to be around those who don't.*

_____

_____

The truth: Of course you deserve respect. Everybody does. If someone is not treating you respectfully, develop a courteous way to assert yourself. Someone with healthy self-esteem has values and recognises that they matter. Consider taking a healthy risk by stepping out of your comfort zone into your stretch zone. You will be respected by others because you dared to speak up for yourself.

People tend to like the easy way out, the person who will sit quietly while they make waves and behave disrespectfully. These types of people (also known as bullies) don't like a challenge. They don't like it when someone stands up to them because it makes their 'job' as a bully more difficult. Let them know if they cross your boundary. You will see how they will move on to the next victim, but that victim will not be you.

What feelings come up for you when you consider standing up for yourself?

_____

_____

_____

Now you have explored some of your limiting beliefs, let's remind ourselves that those beliefs are not you. Can you imagine giving your beliefs a big hug, or showing compassion, the way a mother or father comforts their child? Instead, explore living from your heart and turning a gentle compassionate love towards yourself. If you have trouble knowing how to be compassionate towards yourself, think about how you may feel towards small children and animals. It is the kind of natural unconditional love you need to give yourself.

Design Your Own Life

Now you are aware of some of your limiting beliefs, I am wondering where you want to be in your life? Do you have dreams and aspirations which you are yet to reach or even start working towards? Have you ended up stuck in a job that you hate? Do you approve of the way you're living your life or do you regularly wish things were different?

This type of uncertainty in your lifestyle can easily zap away at your self-esteem, causing you to feel down and even depressed about your life. Can you make a list of the things you want to achieve and start putting together an action plan to get them?

Make it realistic and focus on slow and steady progress and remember those limiting beliefs have no place in your plans.

List your action plans

I will . . .
Example: I will sign up to that salsa lesson.

I can . . .
Example: I can learn to play the guitar.

The above exercise might seem like common sense, however remarkably few of us take the time to visualise our desired future, let alone thinking through the plans we would need to put in place to make that future happen. So, who do you commit to being today?

Takeaways

- Consider how powerful messages have helped or hindered your self-esteem
- Explore ways to reframe messages and instil more self-compassion
- Reflect on your action plans today to begin to make shifts towards building your self-esteem

8 Building Healthy Self-Esteem

When you value yourself and have good enough self-esteem, you feel worthy and you also have positive relationships with others. You begin to feel confident about your abilities, capacities and skills.

People with healthy self-esteem are open to learning and constructive feedback. The exercises you have completed along the way will have supported you to understand how you continually judge and criticise, and how this can be harmful to your self-esteem. You can't always have high levels of self-esteem because life is filled with flaws and imperfections, however, the art of self-care and self-compassion can support you. It takes effort to challenge the habits of a lifetime.

Self-care is something we often overlook, but it's important on many levels. You cannot be there for other people unless you are there for yourself. Why don't you commit to doing the meditation I shared with you over seven days to see how committed you can be to yourself? You cannot be strong for other people unless you look after number one and apply the same strength to you. You cannot realise your dreams and live a more rounded and centred life unless you realise your wants and desires. Yes, sometimes that means focusing on yourself first and foremost.

Susie lived a life where she played it safe. Her father died when she was young and she always had similar interests to her mother and her sister. She enjoyed time away from them but also felt very guilty The message she heard growing up was, 'This is family and we do everything together.' By writing out some of her interests she began to notice the feelings she felt when considering new interests for herself rather than her family.

Like Susie, how many interests have you put off to please others?

Exercise 8.1

What makes you tick?

Can you list twenty things you enjoy doing for yourself?

Here are a few examples: rock-climbing, roller-skating, baking, bike riding, meeting friends, meditating, dancing, knitting, listening to music, horse riding, shopping, walking in the park, volunteering, reading poetry.

_____

_____

_____

_____

_____

_____

_____

_____

_____

I invite you to reflect on the last time you let yourself do something that's on your list. Now let's step into our stretch zone (*see p. 47*) and see if you can make a commitment to yourself and place a date next to a few of them. From the list above, can you write down two things you have avoided that could be done in the next month? This exercise will give you a sense of autonomy and it can support you to acquire and master new skills. You have chosen this book because you are not only wanting a new understanding of your self-esteem, but also the inner freedom to act with more awareness, rather than staying locked in your limiting beliefs.

Example: *I commit to meeting up with three friends in the next four weeks.*

Creativity

Creativity is a wonderful way to boost your feel-good factor because creating something with your hands or with your mind helps you to connect with your inner self.

Try and develop a hobby which is firmly in the creative niche, such as writing, singing, playing a musical instrument, drawing, painting, making something with your hands, baking and cake decorating, or anything which involves you using your creative mind and having something to look at as the final result.

You'll also distract your mind completely from negativity because you're so taken with your new hobby. Who knows, you might even find that you enjoy your new hobby so much that you can make money from it, perhaps selling what you make, such as jewellery, cakes or furniture. Get in contact with your local college for evening or weekend courses; it's a great way to step out of your comfort zone into your stretch zone.

You don't have to sign up for an evening class if you don't want to, although it's a great way to meet new people. Instead, you can take a course at home via the internet, or you can simply read books on subjects you find fascinating.

Reading

How often do you read? The process of reading requires you to slow down and contemplate as opposed to being fast and active to keep up with society's pace. Reading for pleasure for thirty minutes a week can have huge health benefits, including an increase in creativity, greater self-esteem, an improved state of mind, along with an increase of empathy and awareness of general knowledge and cultures. Some of my clients have found it a good idea to try learning a new language, even if it's just the basics – there is nothing more self-esteem-building than being able to speak more than one language. It's another way of stepping out of your comfort zone into your stretch zone.

My Favourite Things

Part of knowing yourself involves re-familiarising yourself with who you truly are. This next process is about getting to know yourself. Not the messages you heard from your parents or grandparents and caregiver, but *your* values, *your* desires and *your* needs.

The following exercise allows you to spend some time thinking about your own identity and getting to know yourself better. I want you to dig deep and share what you like and what your hopes and dreams are. Remember – I'm not asking what your parents or your partners or your siblings want for you. Pay attention to any thoughts that might creep in regarding your expectations, demands or desires of others.

Exercise 8.2

My favourite things

My favourite colour is: _____

Example: *Blue*

Why? _____

Example: *It reminds me of the seaside.*

My favourite food is: _____

Example: *Fish and chips*

Why? _____

Example: *It means Fridays and the end of the week to me,*

My favourite place is: _____

Example: *Grandmother's house*

Why? _____

Example: *I loved her very much and she spoilt me rotten!*

My favourite activity is: _____

Example: *Running*

Why? _____

Example: *It helps me to switch off.*

My favourite hobby or interest is: _____

Example: *Crochet*

Why? _____

Example: *I like to be creative.*

My favourite show, movie or book is: _____

Example: *The Lion King*

Why? _____

Example: *Because of happy childhood memories.*

My dream job would be: _____

Example: *Astronaut*

Why? _____

Example: *I'd love to float above the Earth and look down on it.*

My favourite memories are: _____

Example: *Holidays with my family*

Why? _____

Example: *Laughter*

The German philosopher Frederick Nietzsche once said, 'He who has a why can endure any how.'

If you are wanting to address your levels of self-esteem it is important to understand your *why*. 'Why' is an important step in understanding how you can go for goals, interests and projects that may excite you and in doing so create a life you enjoy living rather than one in which you are simply surviving.

Exercise 8.3
Getting to know your 'why'

By knowing your 'why', you can begin the process of stepping into your stretch zone to take positive risks with yourself.

My greatest accomplishment to date is:

_____

Example: *I saved up and bought my car.*

A defining moment in my life was:

_____

Example: *Graduating from university.*

When I have alone time, I like to:

_____

Example: *Watch Netflix.*

What does it feel like putting these things down on paper? Many people find it difficult to give themselves praise. Many people will have heard it's not good to show off or it's rude to boast. The parental message here is, 'It's okay for others to say how good you are, but not you.' Can you permit yourself to challenge that message? Challenge it and ask yourself why you believe that to be true, why it has to be that way. When you break it down, you'll come to realise that there is no basis for that claim, and you can change it to whatever you want it to be. Remember you are your biggest cheerleader.

Face your Fears

Part of building healthy self-esteem is facing yourself. When you really assess something and pull it apart, you start to diminish its power. It's a little like facing fear because when you question and challenge why you feel the way you do, you see that it's avoidable or it comes down to a choice. This is what you have done by reading this far and my hope is you have managed to tackle some of your challenging questions.

It can be tough to sit down and examine where you are in life in terms of your mental health, your emotional state, and how you generally feel about things, but consider it a form of self-therapy. By being honest with yourself, you're giving yourself the tools to face your situation and overcome it.

Think about the things you want in your life which you have been too scared to go for in the past. How about the job you wanted but never thought about retraining for? How about the relationship you did not attempt because you were too scared of rejection?

Think about these things now and assess whether there is any situation in your life which you could still pursue – it's unlikely to be too late for everything. In that case, give yourself permission to make those healthy choices and go for it.

Have you ever been terrified to do something, absolutely shaking at the thought of it, but then you did it? How did you feel after-wards? Euphoric? Proud of yourself? On top of the world? Probably all of the above.

Doing things that you're scared of not only boosts your self-esteem, but it can also support you to see that you're capable of far more than you realise. If you face your fears it helps you to cast them out of your life. Nothing is as bad as you build it up to be in your mind, and by facing that fear and going for it, you'll see that the fear you have is nothing more than an illusion. That in itself teaches you a very solid and valuable lesson about life.

Exercise 8.4

What's fear got to do with it?

Self-esteem does not mean getting rid of fear. Instead, it is about being able to feel its presence and deciding to move forward anyway.

Jot down some of your fears:

_____

_____

Examples: Failure, Getting it wrong.

Why have you been fearful?

_____

_____

Example: *Not a risk taker.*

What are the excuses you have made to avoid facing a situation or person?

_____

_____

Example: *I won't get it right so it's pointless trying.*

Can you reframe them to sound less scary?

_____

_____

Example: *If I try to take this risk then I can feel different and maybe I can learn from it.*

I have purposefully added these questions about fear at this stage in the book to help you see where you are now on the continuum scale. Can you **Stop**, **Reflect** and **Feel** what is coming up for you and consider the emotions list in Chapter 1? Your fears may still be with you, however it's easier to overcome them and move through them because you are now operating with a stronger sense of purpose, one that can help shift you out of your comfort zone. Are you picking the same ones or are new emotions coming up for you? You have come far in this process of personal development and I am curious to know how much more you know about yourself as compared to after earlier chapters.

Takeaways
- Consider the benefits of having a healthy self-esteem through creativity and reading
- Explore in detail your 'why' and how that affects your purpose and beliefs
- Reflect on how you can work with your fear by expressing it and reframing it

9 Social Media and Anxiety

How much time do you spend on the internet? Many people with low self-esteem will second-guess all the things about themselves that they once knew to be true. We can get so caught up in how other people appear online, we're sent into a cloud of doubt about who we are and what we're passionate about. When you start to compare yourself to what you see on social media, you undermine your own trust in yourself, and this feeds into your low self-esteem.

We may not always realise it but being online plays a huge role in our daily life, and it's certainly something that influences how we view ourselves if we allow it.

Dan came into therapy because he had persistent low self-esteem. Home from university, he had no energy to try new things. He spent a lot of his time online, in particular Instagram and Facebook. This left him feeling worse about himself as he was comparing his insides with other people's outsides.

Many people have been known to spend three hours a day on their smartphones texting, video chatting and browsing the web. Sadly, many lives are divided up into sleeping, working, eating and social media. People with low self-esteem react strongly to social media.

Here is an example of a negative impact that social media can have on your low self-esteem.

When Dan hops on his laptop on a Sunday morning and sees all the fun, upbeat things people have been up to, he feels crappy about his low-key night in.

Social media has people comparing themselves to others. It's important to remember that generally many on social media intentionally put forward the best version of themselves, so what you see isn't ever the whole picture. People facing challenges with their self-esteem tell themselves that there are so many things they're failing at in their life. They question their poor social skills and how socially adept others are at communicating with each other. Feelings of unworthiness are brought up as a result of constantly comparing their lives with others. This was Dan's experience.

I invite you to keep your time online to a minimum and try not to liken yourself and your social skills to anyone else's. There's nobody you have to keep up with. It's not uncommon for people with low self-worth and self-esteem to worry incessantly about their appearance or whether they're 'thin' or 'beautiful' enough to be accepted by society. We only exacerbate these insecurities by constantly flipping through pictures of somewhat attractive people on social media who have probably used some kind of filter to put forth the absolute best image of themselves.

If you spend too much time glued to Instagram (especially celebrity Instagrams, which are chock-full of photoshopped images), this can affect your self-esteem. People with low self-esteem feel 'less than', and this is never a good thing. So try not to stare at other people's images so much, especially if it's going to leave you judging yourself harshly.

Your Appearance

You may be very aware of the main cause for your low self-esteem, and feel that it lies in your perception of your appearance. You were not born with low self-esteem, you were born present and free. Nobody is born disliking, despising or dissatisfied with their appearance. Perhaps there have been times in your past where negative experiences have contributed to how you view yourself. Maybe you were teased about your appearance, or maybe even praised then felt under pressure to continue to be beautiful. Feeling you are bad or thinking you are doing things wrong can cause you to turn against yourself.

Maybe, sadly, there have been violations in your story and rather than be angry with the violator you have blamed yourself. Or you may have witnessed others receiving approval for their appearance and this has led you to believe that if you changed yours then you would get the same approval. You also may have witnessed others being unkind about their own appearance, which then became part of your experience. Sadly, you may have learnt to judge and critique your appearance. If there is no awareness, social media can be seen as part of a hypnotic spell that teaches many to believe that if they look a certain way, they will feel a certain way. Many people believe if they somehow change their appearance they can be more loveable, more seen, more important.

Take the example of Kate on p. 59. Some people may have mixed feelings about themselves because they focus on a particular perceived problem and obsess about it to the point of making themselves feel bad. Kate turned against herself and her appearance. This is probably one of the biggest reasons worldwide for poor self-esteem and I believe we can point the finger in this day and age at social media to some degree and our presence online. It's impossible to try and live up to some perceived perfection that doesn't exist! However, we still try.

I can tell you a million times over that the heart matters more than what you see in the mirror, but if you're down about your weight, your general appearance or anything else, then perhaps you are attempting to tackle that. However, make sure you're only tackling it for you and not to try and fit in with other people or society's messed-up idea of what is attractive and what isn't. We may not have a choice when it comes to our appearance but we do get to choose our thoughts. Challenges with our appearance are only really challenges with our thinking. New and kinder thoughts will support your self-esteem better than the old and critical ones. Concerns with your appearance might be keeping you from addressing deeper pains and I encourage you to look at the further information at the back of the book for further support.

Basic Social Media Rules

I'm not going to sit here and say stop using social media. Some people use it for work, others use it to stay in touch with people they don't see on a regular basis, so it's not the best idea to cut yourself off from the digital world completely. However, there is no doubt that it is possible for social media use to get out of hand. Consider keeping a journal to see how much time you are spending online, and then formulate a plan to bring it under control. Being more mindful of how much time you spend online and making sure that social time remains face-to-face is a great starting point. Perhaps you could find a buddy you can call to help keep you accountable.

Here are some suggestions of starting points if you're ready to protect yourself from the damaging effects of online overload. Remember we are working towards making a conscious choice to be still and mindful.

■ No laptops, tablets or mobiles in the bedroom

Consider moving the charger to another room and avoid charging the phone beside your bed every night. This stops you from checking Facebook or Twitter first and last thing every day. Research has proven the technology itself is bad for you: the light given off by our screens prevents our brains from releasing melatonin, a hormone that tells our bodies it's night-time. Buy an alarm clock!

■ Create a morning ritual

Consider going for a walk, holding a plank, meditating, working out or walking your dog minus your smartphone. All of the above will free your brain up from other things and it's a much better way to start your day.

■ Social time means NO social media

This can be applied when you meet friends for a drink or to watch sports or with family. Surprise yourselves with what happens – out of sight, out of mind! Spark up conversations and commit to having at least one meal a day without your smartphone. Use a stopwatch during the day and not the one on your smartphone. After you have checked your social profiles and have caught up on emails, set it for fifteen minutes and then turn your phone off. By increasing your tech break by five minutes every week or so you will be able to not check in for an hour or more, without getting anxious about what you may have missed.

Why not include some of the practical tips any time throughout the day? For example, you might decide you want to read a book for thirty minutes a day during your lunch break. Or write out your affirmations. Leave your smartphone at your desk when you go for lunch.

Takeaways
- Consider the impact that comparing yourself to others has on your self-esteem
- Explore non-online rituals as a way of reconnecting with yourself
- Reflect on how much social media delivers you powerful messages and how these affect how you see yourself

10 Strategies

We're almost at the end of our book and by now you should be feeling glimmers of hope that you can really start to get your life back on track and feel wonderful about yourself. I am hoping that your journal is bursting with notes and feelings. Self-esteem really can change everything for the better – you simply need to put in the work and the effort to build it up and experience the cumulative effects.

Where are you now on the continuum?

Please don't expect results overnight. This is something which will take time to build up, but when it does, you'll certainly feel a million times better for it! In this final chapter, let's talk about a few strategies you can try to help build up your sense of self-worth, self-esteem and general happiness. Remember, we are working towards 'I'm Okay, You're Okay'.

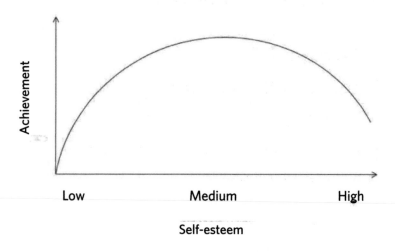

Having healthy self-esteem is not just about blowing your own trumpet but being able to have a realistic view of yourself, which means learning to like and respect yourself – flaws and all. We all have good points and bad points and we all have moments when we know we could act differently, but it's important to accept yourself with these in mind, and not try and ignore them or make yourself feel bad about them.

The Benefits of Healthy Self-Esteem

Exercise 10.1

What are you working towards?

- More resilient and able to tolerate stress and setbacks.

- More assertive in expressing your needs, wants, and opinions.

- More realistic in your expectations.

- More confident in your ability to make decisions.

- More able to form secure, honest relationships.

- More likely to be more compassionate and less overcritical of yourself and others.

- More able to trust your gut and follow your instincts.

- More able to take pride in your accomplishments.

- More able to give yourself credit where credit is due.

- More able to think for yourself.

Circle which of the above you would like to work towards.

By now you will understand that when you are in the grips of low self-esteem, you might find it difficult to bring success or positive thinking to mind. My hope is that given how much you have now invested in yourself you are feeling more upbeat and more open to making changes to your story. Remember, how you feel about yourself is based on your story and you can work towards a positive life position of 'I'm Okay'. Remember, your inner critic has been playing down your importance. Repetition is key if you want to convince and train your brain to think, feel and be .

When you have gained a fair mastery of your emotional states, you can then begin to use positive affirmations, meditation and journalling to boost your self-esteem.

Everyone has successes, achievements and accomplishments in some way, shape or form. You might have to think carefully about them or go through some of the exercises, simply because your inner critic is trying to stop you remembering anything that is considered something to be proud of. You'll certainly find one or two things you're super-proud of so remind yourself why you're so wonderful! Your self-esteem is about your inner you and not your outer you.

Exercise 10.2
Share your successes

Let's get down on paper again things about you such as your sense of humour, being a great listener, your empathy towards others, etc. It can be anything, but it has to be true in your mind and it has to be something that is about *you*, not what others say.

Do you feel you have the courage to share your successes, accomplishments and achievements with a close friend?

What is Important to You?

Take some time to sit down and think about what is important to you. Throughout this book, I have arranged moments for you to **Stop**, **Reflect** and **Feel**. Life has a habit of robbing us of quality time with ourselves and as a result, we lose sight of our values, views, opinions and what is important to us on a deeper level. By spending time thinking about your opinions on certain subjects, and identifying the things which you hold dear, you'll develop inner strength.

It might sound like it's not going to be that effective, but give it a try. The more you build conviction in a particular area, perhaps a strong opinion you have, the stronger you'll feel on the inside. This will have a direct impact on your self-esteem.

Commit to keeping up the journalling for thirty consecutive days, because it's an exercise many find powerful. Having self-compassion is essentially a commitment to self-discipline because it is a daily moment-by-moment practice. Compassion involves recognising the shared human condition – that we all experience moments of feeling flawed and fragile.

Use self-compassion as a guide to recognising that you too have struggles. Try the self-compassion test on Dr Neff's website: www.self-compassion.org.

Declutter

Do a life inventory and work out the things you need versus the things you don't need. Be ruthless here. Take stock of the relationships, things and friendships in your life and understand whether any of them are serving you well. Do you have a particular friend who zaps all your energy, demands all of your time and never does anything for you? All of these will affect your self-esteem. If so, it's time to declutter that friend and focus your time and attention back on you. It's time to declutter that bottom drawer.

By decluttering your life, you'll feel far more in control and your self-esteem will rise as a result. You might think you need the material things in life, and to some degree you do, but you'll also come to realise that experiences, friendships, relationships and the way you feel about yourself are far more fulfilling.

Volunteering

A fast-track route towards feeling good about yourself at times may have nothing to do with you and more to do with others. Your awareness of this can support your self-esteem. Have you considered doing a few good deeds for other people?

Volunteering can give you a sense of purpose. In volunteering, you are supporting your community thus making a difference to something other than yourself. It can give you something meaningful to be doing and it can be empowering to be doing something that does matter.

Volunteering is a great way to meet new people and practise social interactions; remember the stroke theory we discussed? It can also be particularly beneficial if you're feeling isolated and you want to build your social skills or build your confidence around people. Focusing on something else can be a welcome distraction from any negative thoughts about yourself. Can you imagine what it's like knowing people are generally happy to have you around?

When you do a good deed for another person those feel-good chemicals kick in and your level of self-worth increases and others feels good too. All these things are achievable providing you are aware of your boundaries and what you are willing to tolerate.

Takeaways
- Consider how healthy self-esteem can support you to have realistic expectations and more autonomy in your decision-making
- Explore ways to create a different sense of self through volunteering
- Reflect on what is important to you, writing it out daily and applying self-compassion to that process.

Conclusion

And there we have it! You've reached the end of the book.

How do you feel now?

Remember, you're never too old to learn something new, and the whole process of learning gives you something to focus on. The more you learn, the more you succeed and develop new skills, and the more you'll notice that your self-esteem grows. You can't do anything in life, whether you have healthy boundaries in place or you develop a sense of potency unless you give yourself permission to go for things.

You might sit and 'umm' and 'ahh' about something for far too long and as a result, you're left floundering, with the chance totally missed. When you look back you'll start to feel regret, and the 'what if' feeling will stick with you for a long time. The only way to overcome this is to recognise what you're doing and side-step the possible regret by taking action in the here and now.

However, permission has to be total. It's no good doing this in a half-hearted way. Can you own the choices you make and go for them with total commitment? Trusting in yourself is a choice, letting go is a choice; only you can give yourself true permission in the end.

The only thing left to say is good luck. Hopefully, the advice in this book will kickstart you towards a new and fulfilling life, feeling wonderful in yourself. As a result, you'll find many doors begin to open, thanks to this newly discovered level of self-esteem. This is all as a result of recognising your own self-worth and working on your self-esteem.

This is a journey that will be extremely fulfilling on many different levels. There will be times when you think it's not working and you should certainly expect a few days when you feel less than positive, but it's important that you see this as part of the journey and you stick with it. Don't give up simply because you have a down day, or you struggle with one element of your life.

Go back to the exercises and keep up the journalling. We all have sticking points, but that simply means you need to focus on that area a little deeper and work towards overcoming it. Get into the habit of reframing, pay attention to strokes and life positions; you'll feel proud of yourself in the end.

Focus on yourself, give yourself permission to look towards yourself and work on your own life and your own self-esteem in the here and now. Remember, it's not selfish to think about yourself and it's not selfish to put yourself first. Only by focusing on yourself can you become a better version of you, a happier and healthier version who can be there for others, but most importantly can be there for yourself.

Further reading

Berne, E. *Games People Play: The Psychology of Human Relationships*, Penguin (2016 – original work published 1964)

de Board, R. *Counselling for Toads: A Psychological Adventure*, Routledge (1998)

Ernst, F. H., Jr. 'The OK corral: The grid for get-on-with' *Transactional Analysis Journal*, 1(4),33-42 (1971)

Linn, D. *Declutter Your Life as Modern Alchemy*, Hay House (2019)

Neff, K. *Self-compassion: The Proven Power of Being Kind to Yourself*, HarperCollins Publishers Inc (2015)

Rogers, C. *On Becoming a Person*, Constable (2004 – original work published 1954)

Steiner, C. *Scripts People Live: Transactional Analysis of Life Scripts* Grove Press (1990)

Resources

- Association for Contextual Behavioural Science (ACBS) (www.contextualscience.org)

- Breathworks (www.breathworks-mindfulness.org.uk)

- The Happiness Trap (www.thehappinesstrap.com)

- ACT Mindfully (www.actmindfully.com)

- The Compassionate Mind Foundation (www.compassionatemind.co.uk)

- Mindful Self-Compassion UK (www.mindfulselfcompassionuk.com)

- Self-Compassion (www.self-compassion.org)

- The Free Mindfulness Project (www.freemindfulness.org)

- Centre for Mindfulness Research and Practice (www.bangor.ac.uk/mindfulness/)

- Oxford Mindfulness Centre (www.oxfordmindfulness.org)

- Palouse Mindfulness – free online course
  (www.palousemindfulness.com)

- Find a therapist – (www.psychotherapy.org.uk/
  find-a-therapist/)